PAIR
AND
COMPARE

Developing Reading Skills

Geoff Barton
and Mary Bousted

Published by CollinsEducational
An imprint of HarperCollins*Publishers*
77-85 Fulham Palace Road
Hammersmith, London W6 8JB

© HarperCollins*Publishers* 1994
Reprinted 1995

ISBN 0 00 3230430

Geoff Barton and Mary Bousted assert the moral right
to be identified as the authors of this work.

Design by Carla Turchini
Cover design by Wendi Watson
Cover illustration: *Evening* by Alexej von Jawlensky/Bridgeman Art Library

Printed and bound in Great Britain by Scotprint Ltd, Musselburgh

Commissioning editor: Domenica de Rosa
Editor: Rebecca Lloyd
Production: James Graves

CONTENTS

INTRODUCTION

Pair and Compare is an anthology of lively reading materials for use in the classroom. As we were compiling the book, we were told by teachers that what they wanted was a greater variety of texts – non-literary as well as literary materials, contemporary sources alongside pre-twentieth century selections, whole texts and extracts.

We have grouped the material around themes and genres, and our chief purpose is to provide a combative mix of texts in order to provoke discussion, debate and analysis. You will find that texts relating to similar subjects are placed side by side, but that their authors often take radically opposed views. This should lead to some lively classwork.

READING SKILLS

We are also keen that the anthology should help teachers to focus on specific aspects of reading, hence our subtitle. We do not see the reading process as a narrowly mechanistic one, in which pupils tick off one skill and move on to the next, but we do recognize that teachers increasingly need to focus precisely on what pupils need to practise. The skills we are concerned with in *Pair and Compare* are:

1 Developing personal response
2 Reading for meaning
3 Reading aloud
4 Seeking information
5 Identifying key points
6 Summarising
7 Scanning/skimming
8 Distinguishing fact from fiction/detecting bias
9 Analysing language
10 Studying genre

Our list of reading skills is not narrowly tied to the National Curriculum for English. Instead, it is a list of the skills and experiences which we believe pupils need to develop in order to become confident and effective readers. To support the teacher we have ensured that our activities focus on specific skills. We have not included 'reading for pleasure' as a reading skill because we see it as fundamental to our entire selection.

USING THE BOOK

Pair and Compare is arranged in nine units, each covering a particular theme. Within each unit, texts are placed in pairs, or in larger groups, and occasionally one text stands alone. After each text, you will find short 'After Reading' questions which aim to take children *back into* the text and deepen their understanding. Sometimes there are also 'Before Reading' questions. Following each group of texts is a 'Compare' section containing longer 'Discussion' and 'Assignment' questions. These aim to help children think more carefully about the language and, finally, to take them *beyond* the text – to examine wider issues and principles.

We have aimed to ensure a variety of responses to texts, encouraging pupils to discuss what they have read in groups, to analyse, think and rethink, and write about their conclusions.

PRE-TWENTIETH CENTURY LITERATURE

We have sought pieces of earlier writing which really work in class, making them rub shoulders with contemporary extracts on similar themes. Our belief here is that the content will provide pupils with a way into the text – an initial point of comparison before they move on to look more closely at the writer's language. We think pre-twentieth century literature is important not because it was written in the past, but because it has something distinctive to say – and this has been our chief criterion for selection.

DIFFERENTIATION

This is a book for pupils of all abilities. We have included accessible texts alongside very demanding ones, and aimed to provide activities and approaches which will support pupils working at all levels. The suggested activities always provide for a wide degree of differentiation, and we suggest that you guide pupils to the assignment most appropriate to their interests and abilities.

CONCLUSION

We hope that you will find *Pair and Compare* a source of lively and stimulating lesson materials, and that the layout proves attractive and easy to use. The companion book for Key Stage 3, *Pair and Compare 1*, provides a further range of texts and resources to provoke debate and analysis with younger pupils. Sharp analysis, informed discussion and encounters with demanding texts should begin as early as possible.

GEOFF BARTON
MARY BOUSTED

HOW THE OTHER HALF LIVES

There must be very few people who have not dreamed about being rich and powerful. Many happy day-dreams are based on a vision of being able to buy all the things we desire, or being able to get what we want by ordering other people about.
- *Are rich and powerful people different from ordinary mortals?*
- *Why do we find the lives of the rich and the famous so fascinating?*
- *What standards of behaviour do we expect from those who govern us?*

THE RICH ARE DIFFERENT

■ Lives of the rich are described in these three novel extracts – two set in England and one in America.

READING SKILLS
Identifying key points
Analysing language

THE GO-BETWEEN

Breakfast at Brandham Hall started with family prayers at nine o'clock. These were read by Mr Maudsley sitting at the head of the table (all the dishes were on the sideboard). The chairs were drawn back and ranged round the walls; they were all alike, I think, but I had my favourite chair which I could distinguish by certain signs and I always tried to get it. After the gong had gone the servants filed in headed by the butler wearing his most solemn air. I always counted them but could never make them more than ten, though there were said to be twelve in the house. The family were less regular in attendance. Mrs Maudsley was always there; Marcus and I made it a point of honour; Denys came from time to time and Marian, who was seldom there at the opening, sometimes came in half-way through. On the whole, rather more than half the guests used to attend. It was in no way compulsory, Marcus told me; but most households that were not 'fast' had family prayers (I dared not tell him that ours hadn't). His father rather liked one to go, but would not be angry if one didn't.

First we sat, then we turned round and knelt down. While we were sitting was the best time to make observations, to study the guests, or, which was easier, the servants, for they sat opposite to us. Marcus was to some extent in their confidence; he knew, for instance, which of them had been getting into trouble, and why. If one of them could be thought of as looking red-eyed, it lent a touch of drama to the morning ceremony. Afterwards, kneeling, one could press one's knuckles into one's eyes to make the colours come, and one could observe intensely over a very restricted field of vision. Covertly to extend this, without incurring the charge of irreverence, was one of the tasks one set oneself.

This morning, my first Sunday morning at Brandham Hall, Marcus did not come down with me. He said he didn't feel well. He did not, as I should have, debate with himself whether he should get up or not or ask anyone's leave to stay in bed; he just stayed there. His pale cheeks were a little flushed and his eyes bright. 'Don't worry about me,' he said. 'Someone will come. Give Trimingham my kind regards.'

Secretly resolving to tell Mrs Maudsley as soon as prayers were over (for apart from real concern for his state I fancied myself as a breaker of bad news) I waited for the last stroke of the gong and presently found myself at the head of the double staircase. I had no difficulty in remembering which track to take....

The men walked about to eat their porridge. This, Marcus told me, was *de rigueur*; only cads ate their porridge sitting down. I roamed about with mine, fearful of spilling it. The ladies, however, remained seated. Mrs Maudsley seemed preoccupied. Her inscrutable, beeline glance rested several times on Trimingham – it didn't have to travel, it was *there*. But it never turned my way, and when at last I did get her attention the meal was over, we were leaving the table, and she said: 'Oh, isn't Marcus here?' She hadn't even noticed that he wasn't, although he was such a favourite with her. But she went straight up to his room, where, after making sure the coast was clear, I followed her. To my astonishment I found an envelope with 'No Admittance' on it fixed with two drawing pins to our door. This was a challenge I at once took up: besides, it was my room as well as Marcus's, and no one had the right to keep me out. I opened the door and put my head in.

'What's up?' I said.

'It was decent of you to trickle along,' said Marcus languidly from the bed, 'but don't come in. I have a headache and some spots and Mama thinks it may be measles. She didn't say so, but I know.'

'Hard cheese, old man,' I said. 'But what about the jolly old quarantine?'

'Well, cases do develop when it's over. But the doctor's coming, and he'll know. What fun for you if you get it. Perhaps we shall all get it, like at school. Then we shan't be able to have the cricket match or the ball or anything. Lord, I shall laugh!'

'Is there to be a cricket match?'

'Yes, we have it every year. It helps to keep them quiet.'

'And a ball?' I asked, apprehensively. I didn't feel equal to a ball.

'Yes, that's for Marian, and Trimingham, and all the neighbours. It's to be on Saturday the 28th. Mama's sent out the invitations. Cripes! The place will be a hospital by then!'

We both laughed like hyenas at the prospect, and Marcus said, 'You'd better not stay here breathing in my ruddy germs.'

'Oh God, perhaps you're right. That reminds me, I want my prayer-book.'

'What, are you going to the jolly old kirk?'

'Well, I thought I might.'

'Pretty decent of you, but you needn't, you know.'

'No, but I don't want to let the side down. We do it at home sometimes,' I told him, tolerantly. 'Shall I slink across the room and get my prayer-buggins?'

Last term it had been the fashion to call a book a 'buggins'.

'Yes, but hold your breath.'

I filled my lungs, dashed to the chest of drawers, snatched the prayer-book, and scarlet in the face regained the door.

'Good egg, I didn't think you could,' said Marcus, while I gasped. 'And have you got any old button or such-like for the collection?'

Again the under-water dash to the chest of drawers but this time I had to come up for air. As I gulped it down I had a distinct feeling of several germs, the size of gnats, going down my windpipe. To distract myself I opened my purse and sniffed it. The new leather had a pungent, aromatic smell almost as reviving as a smelling-bottle; and the central partition, which opened with a thief-proof catch, sheltered a half-sovereign. Other partitions had other coins, arranged in order of value; the outermost held pennies.

'Mama would give you something if you asked her,' Marcus said. 'She probably will anyhow. She's decent about that.'

An access of masculine secrecy about money suddenly stopped my tongue.

'I'll think it over,' I said, pinching the purse which crackled deliciously.

'Well, don't break the bank. So long, old chap. Don't pray too hard.'

'Ta-ta, you old shammer,' I replied.

At home we had one way of talking and at school another: they were distinct as two different languages. But when we were alone together, and especially when any excitement – like Marcus's suspected measles – was afoot, we often lapsed into schoolboy talk, even away from school. Only when Marcus was instructing me in *les convenances*, as he called them, for he liked to air his French, did he stick closely to an unadorned vocabulary. They were a serious matter.

L P HARTLEY

AFTER READING

1 What do we learn about Marcus's family?

2 Does Leo feel 'at home' in Marcus's house? Explain your answer.

■ In this extract, Gatsby's neighbour describes the start of one of Gatsby's famous parties.

The Great Gatsby

There was music from my neighbor's house through the summer nights. In his blue gardens men and girls came and went like moths among the whisperings and the champagne and the stars. At high tide in the afternoon I watched his guests diving from the tower of his raft, or taking the sun on the hot sand of his beach while his two motor-boats slit the waters of the Sound, drawing aquaplanes over cataracts of foam. On week-ends his Rolls-Royce became an omnibus, bearing parties to and from the city between nine in the morning and long past midnight, while his station wagon scampered like a brisk yellow bug to meet all trains. And on

Mondays eight servants, including an extra gardener, toiled all day with mops and scrubbing-brushes and hammers and garden shears, repairing the ravages of the night before.

Every Friday five crates of oranges and lemons arrived from a fruiterer in New York – every Monday these same oranges and lemons left his back door in a pyramid of pulpless halves. There was a machine in the kitchen which could extract the juice of two hundred oranges in half an hour if a little button was pressed two hundred times by a butler's thumb.

At least once a fortnight a corps of caterers came down with several hundred feet of canvas and enough colored lights to make a Christmas tree of Gatsby's enormous garden. On buffet tables, garnished with glistening hors-d'oeuvre, spiced baked hams crowded against salads of harlequin designs and pastry pigs and turkeys bewitched to a dark gold. In the main hall a bar with a real brass rail was set up, and stocked with gins and liquors and with cordials so long forgotten that most of his female guests were too young to know one from another.

By seven o'clock the orchestra has arrived, no thin five-piece affair, but a whole pitful of oboes and trombones and saxophones and viols and cornets and piccolos, and low and high drums. The last swimmers have come in from the beach now and are dressing upstairs; the cars from New York are parked five deep in the drive, and already the halls and salons and verandas are gaudy with primary colors, and hair shorn in strange new ways, and shawls beyond the dreams of Castile. The bar is in full swing, and floating rounds of cocktails permeate the garden outside, until the air is alive with chatter and laughter, and casual innuendo and introductions forgotten on the spot, and enthusiastic meetings between women who never knew each other's names.

The lights grow brighter as the earth lurches away from the sun, and now the orchestra is playing yellow cocktail music, and the opera of voices pitches a key higher. Laughter is easier minute by minute, spilled with prodigality, tipped out at a cheerful word. The groups change more swiftly, swell with new arrivals, dissolve and form in the same breath; already there are wanderers, confident girls who weave here and there among the stouter and more stable, become for a sharp, joyous moment the centre of a group, and then, excited with triumph, glide on through the sea-change of faces and voices and color under the constantly changing light.

Suddenly one of these gypsies, in trembling opal, seizes a

cocktail out of the air, dumps it down for courage and, moving her hands like Frisco, dances out alone on the canvas platform. A momentary hush; the orchestra leader varies his rhythm obligingly for her, and there is a burst of chatter as the erroneous news goes around that she is Gilda Gray's understudy from the *Follies*. The party has begun.

I believe that on the first night I went to Gatsby's house I was one of the few guests who had actually been invited. People were not invited – they went there. They got into automobiles which bore them out to Long Island, and somehow they ended up at Gatsby's door. Once there they were introduced by somebody who knew Gatsby, and after that they conducted themselves according to the rules of behavior associated with amusement parks. Sometimes they came and went without having met Gatsby at all, came for the party with a simplicity of heart that was its own ticket of admission.

F SCOTT FITZGERALD

AFTER READING

1 Look closely at the first three paragraphs. Make a list of all the work that has to be done to organise one of Gatsby's parties.

2 Why is the reader given this information?

■ Bertie Wooster and his long-suffering manservant, Jeeves, disagree about matters of dress.

Right Ho, Jeeves

I don't know if you were at Cannes this summer. If you were, you will recall that anybody with any pretensions to being the life and soul of the party was accustomed to attend binges at the Casino in the ordinary evening-wear trouserings topped to the north by a white mess jacket with brass buttons. And ever since I had stepped aboard the Blue Train at Cannes station, I had been wondering on and off how mine would go with Jeeves.

In the matter of evening costume, you see, Jeeves is hidebound and reactionary. I had had trouble with him before about soft-bosomed shirts. And while these mess jackets had, as I say, been all the rage – *tout ce qu'il y a de chic* – on the Côte d'Azur, I had never concealed it

from myself, even when treading the measure at the Palm Beach Casino in the one I had hastened to buy, that there might be something of an upheaval about it on my return.

I prepared to be firm.

'Yes, Jeeves?' I said. And though my voice was suave, a close observer in a position to watch my eyes would have noticed a steely glint. Nobody has a greater respect for Jeeves's intellect than I have, but this disposition of his to dictate to the hand that fed him had got, I felt, to be checked. This mess jacket was very near to my heart, and I jolly well intended to fight for it with all the vim of great old Sieur de Wooster at the Battle of Agincourt.

'Yes, Jeeves?' I said. 'Something on your mind, Jeeves?'

'I fear that you inadvertently left Cannes in the possession of a coat belonging to some other gentleman, sir.'

I switched on the steely a bit more.

'No, Jeeves,' I said, in a level tone, 'the object under advisement is mine. I bought it out there.'

'You wore it, sir?'

'Every night.'

'But surely you are not proposing to wear it in England, sir?'

I saw that we had arrived at the nub.

'Yes, Jeeves.'

'But, sir -'

'You were saying, Jeeves?'

'It is quite unsuitable, sir.'

'I do not agree with you, Jeeves. I anticipate a great popular success for this jacket. It is my intention to spring it on the public tomorrow at Pongo Twistleton's birthday party, where I confidently expect it to be one long scream from start to finish. No argument, Jeeves. No discussion. Whatever fantastic objection you may have taken to it, I wear this jacket.'

'Very good, sir.'

He went on with his unpacking. I said no more on the subject. I had won the victory, and we Woosters do not triumph over a beaten foe. Presently, having completed my toilet, I bade the man a cheery farewell and in generous mood suggested that, as I was dining out, why didn't he take the evening off and go to some improving picture or something. Sort of olive branch, if you see what

I mean.

He didn't seem to think much of it.

'Thank you, sir, I will remain in.' I surveyed him narrowly.

'Is this dudgeon, Jeeves?'

'No, sir, I am obliged to remain on the premises. Mr Fink-Nottle informed me he would be calling to see me this evening.'

'Oh, Gussie's coming, is he? Well, give him my love.'

'Very good, sir.'

'And a whisky and soda, and so forth.'

'Very good, sir.'

'Right ho, Jeeves.'

I then set off for the Drones.

P G WODEHOUSE

AFTER READING

1 Do Jeeves and Bertie Wooster have a typical master/servant relationship?

2 P G Wodehouse has been described as a 'comic genius'. Do you find his characters amusing? Give reasons for your view.

COMPARE

Discussion

1 How do we know that the characters in *The Go-Between*, *The Great Gatsby* and *Right Ho, Jeeves* are very rich? In pairs, find evidence from the passages to support your view.

2 What is your opinion of the people described in each of the passages? What words would you use to describe them and the lives that they lead? Do you like them? Would you want to be like them? Give reasons for your opinions, then compare them with your partner's.

3 Which passages are set in England and which in America? How can you tell?

Assignments

1 What do the characters in the passages have in common, and what is different about them, and the way that they lead their lives? Back up each comparison that you make with evidence from the texts.

2 Look closely at the following phrases from *The Great Gatsby*. What picture is the author trying to create in the reader's mind?

- In his blue gardens men and girls came and went like moths
- salads of harlequin designs
- wanderers...glide on through the sea-change of faces and color under the constantly changing light.

3 Leo and Marcus in *The Go-Between* speak a type of English widely used by the upper classes before the war. Leo and Marcus also use schoolboy slang. Look closely at their conversation, from 'What's up?', and make a list of the words which you think are slang. Then, rewrite the conversation as if you were talking to a friend, adding modern slang where appropriate. Compare the impressions conveyed by the original conversation and by your modern version.

WHO'S IN THE NEWS?

The rich and the famous are much more likely than 'ordinary' people to be mentioned in the press. From your reading of newspapers and magazines discuss:

- What do 'ordinary' people have to do to be reported in newspapers and magazines?
- Why are people so keen to read about the rich and the famous?

READING SKILLS

Scanning/skimming

Studying genre

■ Prince William is the subject of this extract from a newspaper article, while the following three short articles deal with 'ordinary' people.

A CRYING SHAME

Why William, the boy from a broken home, shed tears on his way back to school.

by PENNY WARK

I N A WEEKEND when Prince Charles seemed to be working hard to be seen as a caring father, Prince William's tears might just have been to his dad's advantage.

The tears which marked the 11-year-old prince's farewell to his adored father were genuine enough, and created a photo opportunity that was unusual for not being stage-managed.

The skiing holiday with daddy had been fun and now William had only the emotional cool of boarding school to anticipate. He would not see his father until Easter and like many other children he could not stop himself from crying as playtime ended and separation began.

His reaction does not seem surprising until you consider that William has been brought up in an emotionally stunted family. He has been trained to display only control in public, and his embarrassment at losing that control showed as he turned away from the cameras to hide his tears.

Something had pushed him too far. Was it just his natural sadness at leaving the father he rarely sees and returning to the formal regime of school? Did the farewell remind him painfully of his parents' separation?

Or were his tears the result of a more complex situation in which his parents, perhaps inadvertently, use him and Harry as public proof that each is a wonderful human being and loving parent?

Diana has done it with countless private visits to Thorpe Park and exotic foreign beaches. The photographers line up, Diana tosses back her head in ecstasy, the boys squeal with excitement and the world gets the message that this is a happy family at play.

And last year it looked as if Charles was determined to prove he was a relaxed father by romping with his sons at Balmoral.

The recent skiing holiday was similarly full of jolly moments of father-and-son togetherness.

At 11, William is old enough to understand that being photographed is part of his lot and old enough to read newspapers' comments on his parents' manoeuvres.

And as he hovers uneasily between childhood and adolescence, he will be acutely sensitive to strained atmospheres. In his case these arise when his father, never a natural performer, poses for photographers.

Like other children of his age, William's reactions can be both frighteningly grown-up and oddly babyish, says psychologist Dorothy Rowe.

"When you've had a lovely holiday and you've got to go back to school is seems so unfair at the time. Some of the tears were for that," she comments.

TODAY

KNIFE FIEND BLOWN AWAY

Ninety-year-old Albert Goodall scared off a knife fiend ransacking his home – by blowing a whistle on him.

Albert grabbed the whistle after he grappled with the raider and was knocked to the ground.

The intruder, who had pushed his way in, fled after cutting Albert's hand.

Albert, of Farnley, Leeds said: "I gave an almighty blow. The whole street must have heard."

THE SUN

BINGO £10,000 HAS MAVIS MIGRATING

By Brandon Malinsky

MUM Mavis Smith scooped £10,000 on The Sun's Great British Bingo yesterday and trilled: "Now I can flutter off on holiday to the Canaries!"

Mavis, who wins half our £20,000 jackpot, will take hubby Philip, 56, to the sunshine isle of Fuerteventura.

She toasted her success with champagne and said:

"This is a gift from God. I've been doing Sun Bingo since it started but I never though this would happen to me."

Mavis, who has a daughter Tracey, 30, called house on number 74 in Game 76.

The former Telecom factory worker, of Yardley Wood, Birmingham, shares the jackpot with Sylvia Farrant, 79.

Sylvia, of Farnborough, Hants, plans to visit relatives in Australia.

THE SUN

HONESTY'S A WINNER

Jobless Bridget Gaskell picked up a £1,500 cheque yesterday – and proved honesty pays.

Bridget, 33, found £29,000 from a robbery in the street and handed it to police.

The cash had been seized from a film company in Brighton.

Bridget, from Brighton, was also presented with free travel and theatre tickets by London Films. She said: "I'm thrilled."

THE SUN

AFTER READING

1 Scan through all the reports. Which has the most interesting headline?

2 Are all the reports as interesting as their headlines promise?

COMPARE

Discussion

1 Scan through the articles written about ordinary people who have experienced something extraordinary. What similarities do you find between these articles?

2 Which of the two types of report (either about the 'Royals' or the 'ordinary' people) did you think was the most interesting and why?

3 Discuss any ways you can see in which the newspapers try to make us like the people they describe. Which words are used to gain our sympathy?

Assignments

1 Compare the article 'A Crying Shame' with one of the other articles in this section. Reread both articles and answer the following questions:

- Which report has the more eye-catching headline? Give reasons for your view.
- Look at the opening sentence of each report. Which gives the more factual information?
- Pick out two words used to describe Prince William and two which describe the 'ordinary' person. What impression of each person are you meant to gain from the use of these words?
- What other differences can you find between the two reports?

2 Look again at the article 'A Crying Shame'. In your opinion, is it fair to write this sort of article about an eleven-year-old boy? Discuss this question with the other pupils in your class, considering in particular the following points:

- How much of the article is hard fact, and how much of it is opinion?
- Is this a fair report about a matter of national interest?

Then write a letter to the editor of the newspaper expressing your point of view about this article.

3 Write your own short article about an 'ordinary' person who has had an extraordinary experience. Try to write it in the style of the articles that you have read.

THE RULERS AND THE RULED

■ The following three poems are about rulers in different countries. What personal qualities do we expect of our governors? What can we do when they do not use their power wisely and well?

Shelley wrote this sonnet after a visit to the British Museum, where he saw some Egyptian relics, notably a huge statue of the Emperor Rameses II.

Ozymandias

I met a traveller from an antique land

Who said: Two vast and trunkless legs of stone

Stand in the desert...Near them, on the sand,

Half sunk, a shattered visage lies, whose frown,

And wrinkled lip, and sneer of cold command,

Tell that its sculptor well those passions read

Which yet survive, stamped on these lifeless things,

The hand that mocked them, and the heart that fed:

And on the pedestal these words appear:

'My name is Ozymandias, king of kings:

Look on my works, ye Mighty, and despair!'

Nothing beside remains. Round the decay

Of that colossal wreck, boundless and bare,

The lone and level sands stretch far away.

1 Imagine that you had seen the statue and were describing it to someone. What would you say about it?

2 Look carefully at the name 'Ozymandias'. In pairs, discuss what you think it could mean.

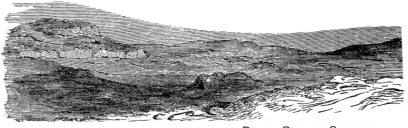

PERCY BYSSHE SHELLEY

■ The next poem is from Ghana.

Admonition to a Chief

Tell him that
We do not wish for greediness
We do not wish that he should curse us
We do not wish that his ears should be
hard of hearing
We do not wish that he should call people fools
We do not wish that he should act
on his own initiative
We do not wish things done as in Kumasi
We do not wish that it should ever be said
'I have no time, I have no time'
We do not wish personal abuse
We do not wish personal violence.

ANON

1 Why are the words 'We do not wish' repeated in the poem?

2 Why should the ruler never say 'I have no time' ?

■ The final poem is from Nigeria.

Olorum Nimbe

I am greeting you, Mayor of Lagos,
Mayor of Lagos, Olorum Nimbe,
Look after Lagos carefully.
As we pick up a yam pounder with care,
As we pick up a grinding stone with care,
As we pick up a child with care,
So may you handle Lagos with care.

ANON

1 What words are repeated in this poem, and what is the effect of the repetition?

2 What do you think the expression 'Olorum Nimbe' could mean?

COMPARE

Discussion

1   In pairs, decide what you consider to be the main point of each of the three poems.

What messages about leadership do they have in common? How do they differ?

2   Which poem did you find most interesting? Give reasons for your view.

3   If you ruled the country for a day, what three laws would you pass to make it a better place for all to live? Share your views with the rest of the class.

4   Who rules your life or has power over you? Which aspects of their authority do you accept and which do you reject?

Assignments

1   What does the description of the statue of Ozymandias with 'wrinkled lip and sneer of cold command' tell you about him? What other clues can you find in the sonnet which tell you more about the type of person this ruler was?

2   Make a list of the qualities that each African poet is looking for in a ruler.

3   Compare your answers to Assignment 1 with those of Assignment 2. Would the African poets want Ozymandias to be their ruler? Give reasons for your view.

4   When the statue of Ozymandias was first built, what effect do you think it was supposed to have on those who saw it? Did it have this effect on the traveller who saw it in the desert? What points do you think the author is making about rulers in this poem?

WIDER READING

Rags-to-Riches Stories
Arnold Bennett, *The Card*; Barbara Taylor Bradford, *A Woman of Substance*; Jeffrey Archer, *Kane and Abel*; John Braine, *Room at the Top*.

Rags-to-Riches Biographies & Autobiographies
Keith Todd, *Kevin Costner: The Unauthorized Biography*; John McCabe, *Charlie Chaplin*; Ray Coleman, *John Lennon*; Shirley Temple Black, *Autobiography*; Brian Blessed, *The Dynamite Kid*; Michael Caine, *What's It All About?*

AFTER READING

1 From your reading of the 'rags-to-riches' stories and the biographies, define what qualities people who want to be rich and famous need to develop in order to achieve this ambition.

2 Write a parody of a 'rags-to-riches' story. Remember that however you exaggerate the characters and the plot, your parody must have enough similarities to the true 'rags-to-riches' genre to enable your readers to "see the joke".

HORROR

Some people enjoy being frightened – think of roller-coasters, ghost stories and horror films. Is it morbid fascination with death and horror? Or it is a way of coping with our deepest fears?
- *Why do people find horror stories and films so fascinating?*
- *What are the classic ingredients of a horror story?*

CLASSIC HORROR

■ The three horror stories which follow were all written more than a hundred years ago.

Mary Shelley wrote *Frankenstein* in 1798, as the result of a challenge from her husband to see who could write a better horror story. In this extract, the monster has escaped after committing murder, and his creator, Dr Frankenstein, meets him again in the Alps.

READING SKILLS

Reading for meaning

Analysing language

Developing personal response

FRANKENSTEIN

IT WAS NEARLY NOON when I arrived at the top of the ascent. For some time I sat upon the rock that overlooks the sea of ice. A mist covered both that and the surrounding mountains. Presently a breeze dissipated the cloud, and I descended upon the glacier. The surface is very uneven, rising like the waves of a troubled sea, descending low, and interspersed by rifts that sink deep. The field of ice is almost a league in width, but I spent nearly two hours in crossing it. The opposite mountain is a bare perpendicular rock. From the side where I now stood Montanvert was exactly opposite, at the distance of a league; and above it rose Mont Blanc, in awful majesty. I remained in a recess of the rock, gazing on this wonderful and stupendous scene. The sea, or rather the vast river of ice, wound among its dependent mountains, whose aerial summits hung over its recesses. Their icy and glittering peaks shone in the sunlight over the clouds. My heart, which was before sorrowful, now swelled with something like joy; I exclaimed – 'Wandering spirits, if indeed ye wander, and do not rest in your narrow beds, allow me this faint happiness or take me, as your companion, away from the joys of life.'

As I said this I suddenly beheld the figure of a man, at some distance, advancing towards me with superhuman speed. He bounded over the crevices in the ice, among

which I had walked with caution; his stature, also, as he approached, seemed to exceed that of man. I was troubled; a mist came over my eyes, and I felt a faintness seize me; but I was quickly restored by the cold gale of the mountains. I perceived, as the shape came nearer (sight tremendous and abhorred!) that it was the wretch whom I had created. I trembled with rage and horror, resolving to wait his approach and then close with him in mortal combat. He approached; his countenance bespoke bitter anguish, combined with disdain and malignity, while its unearthly ugliness rendered it almost too horrible for human eyes. But I scarcely observed this; rage and hatred had at first deprived me of utterance, and I recovered only to overwhelm him with words expressive of furious detestation and contempt.

'Devil,' I exclaimed, 'do you dare approach me? And do not you fear the fierce vengeance of my arm wreaked on your miserable head? Begone, vile insect! Or rather, stay, that I may trample you to dust! And, oh! That I could, with the extinction of your miserable existence, restore those victims whom you have so diabolically murdered!'

'I expected this reception,' said the daemon. 'All men hate the wretched; how, then, must I be hated, who am miserable beyond all living things! Yet you, my creator, detest and spurn me, thy creature, to whom thou art bound by ties only dissoluble by the annihilation of one of us. You purpose to kill me. How dare you sport thus with life? Do your duty towards me, and I will do mine towards you and the rest of mankind. If you will comply with my conditions, I will leave them and you at peace; but if you refuse, I will glut the maw of death, until it be satiated with the blood of your remaining friends.'

'Abhorred monster! Fiend that thou art! The tortures of hell are too mild a vengeance for thy crimes. Wretched devil! You reproach me with your creation; come on, then, that I may extinguish the spark which I so negligently bestowed.'

MARY SHELLEY

AFTER READING

1 What does the monster want from Dr Frankenstein?

2 In what ways is the *Frankenstein* story different from any film versions you may have seen? Look in particular at the character of the monster.

■ 'The Raven' is a nineteenth-century horror story written in verse. How does the poetic form affect the horror?

The Raven

Once upon a midnight dreary, while I pondered, weak and weary,
Over many a quaint and curious volume of forgotten lore –
While I nodded, nearly napping, suddenly there came a tapping,
As of some one gently rapping, rapping at my chamber door.
''Tis some visitor,' I muttered, 'tapping at my chamber door –
       Only this and nothing more.'

Ah, distinctly I remember it was in the bleak December;
And each separate dying ember wrought its ghost upon the floor.
Eagerly I wished the morrow; – vainly I had sought to borrow
From my books surcease of sorrow – sorrow for the lost Lenore
For the rare and radiant maiden whom the angels name Lenore –
                              Nameless <u>here</u> for evermore.

And the silken, sad, uncertain rustling of each purple curtain
Thrilled me – filled me with fantastic terrors never felt before;
So that now, to still the beating of my heart, I stood repeating
''Tis some visitor entreating entrance at my chamber door –
Some late visitor entreating entrance at my chamber door; –
                              This it is and nothing more.'

Presently my soul grew stronger; hesitating then no longer,
'Sir,' said I, 'or Madam, truly your forgiveness I implore;
But the fact is I was napping, and so gently you came rapping,
And so faintly you came tapping, tapping at my chamber door,
That I scarce was sure I heard you' – here I opened wide the door; –
                              Darkness there and nothing more.

Deep into that darkness peering, long I stood there wondering, fearing,
Doubting, dreaming dreams no mortal ever dared to dream before;
But the silence was unbroken, and the stillness gave no token,
And the only word there spoken was the whispered word, 'Lenore!'
This I whispered, and an echo murmured back the word 'Lenore!'
                              Merely this and nothing more.

Back into the chamber turning, all my soul within me burning,
Soon again I heard a tapping somewhat louder than before.
'Surely,' said I, 'surely that is something at my window lattice;
Let me see, then, what thereat is, and this mystery explore –
Let my heart be still a moment and this mystery explore; –
                              'Tis the wind and nothing more!'

Open here I flung the shutter, when, with many a flirt and flutter
In there stepped a stately Raven of the saintly days of yore.
Not the least obeisance made he; not a minute stopped or stayed he;
But, with mein of lord or lady, perched above my chamber door –
Perched upon a bust of Pallas just above my chamber door –
                              Perched, and sat, and nothing more.

Then this ebony bird beguiling my sad fancy into smiling,
By the grave and stern decorum of the countenance it wore,
'Though thy crest be shorn and shaven, thou,' I said, 'are sure no craven,
Ghastly grim and ancient Raven wandering from the Nightly shore –
Tell me what thy lordly name is on the Night's Plutonian shore!'
                              Quoth the Raven, 'Nevermore.'

Much I marvelled this ungainly fowl to hear discourse so plainly,
Though its answer little meaning – little relevancy bore;
For we cannot help agreeing that no living human being
Ever yet was blessed with seeing bird above his chamber door –
Bird or beast upon the sculptured bust above his chamber door,
                              With such name as 'Nevermore.'

But the Raven, sitting lonely on the placid bust, spoke only
That one word, as if his soul in that one word he did outpour.
Nothing farther then he uttered – not a feather then he fluttered –
Till I scarcely more than muttered 'Other friends have flown before –
On the morrow he will leave me, as my hopes have flown before.'
                              Then the bird said 'Nevermore.'

Startled at the stillness broken by reply so aptly spoken,
'Doubtless,' said I, 'what it utters is its only stock and store
Caught from some unhappy master whom unmerciful Disaster
Followed fast and followed faster till his songs one burden bore –
Till the dirges of his Hope that melancholy burden bore
                              Of "Never – nevermore."'

But the Raven still beguiling all my fancy into smiling,
Straight I wheeled a cushioned seat in front of bird, and bust and door;
Then, upon the velvet sinking, I betook myself to linking
Fancy unto fancy, thinking what this ominous bird of yore –
What this grim, ungainly, ghastly, gaunt, and ominous bird of yore
                                 Meant in croaking 'Nevermore.'

This I sat engaged in guessing, but no syllable expressing
To the fowl whose fiery eyes now burned into my bosom's core;
This and more I sat divining, with my head at ease reclining
On the cushion's velvet lining that the lamp-light gloated o'er,
But whose velvet violet lining with the lamp-light gloating o'er;
                                 <u>She</u> shall press, ah, nevermore!

Then, methought, the air grew denser, perfumed from an unseen censer
Swung by Seraphim whose foot-falls tinkled on the tufted floor.
'Wretch,' I cried, 'thy God hath lent thee – by these angels he hath sent thee
Respite – respite and nepenthe – from thy memories of Lenore;
Quaff, oh quaff this kind nepenthe and forget this lost Lenore!'
                                 Quoth the Raven, 'Nevermore.'

'Prophet!' said I, 'thing of evil! prophet still, if bird or devil! –
Whether Tempter sent, or whether tempest tossed thee here ashore,
 Desolate yet all undaunted, on this desert land enchanted –
On this home by Horror haunted – tell me truly, I implore –
Is there – is there balm in Gilead? – tell me – tell me, I implore!'
                                 Quoth the Raven 'Nevermore.'

'Prophet!' said I, 'thing of evil! – prophet still, if bird or devil!
By that Heaven that bends above us – by that God we both adore –
Tell this soul with sorrow laden if, within the distant Aidenn,
It shall clasp a sainted maiden whom the angels name Lenore –
Clasp a rare and radiant maiden whom the angels name Lenore.'
                                 Quoth the Raven 'Nevermore.'

'Be that word our sign of parting, bird or fiend!' I shrieked, up starting –
'Get thee back into the tempest and the Night's Plutonian shore!
Leave no black plume as a token of that lie thy soul hath spoken!
Leave my loneliness unbroken! – quit the bust above my door!
Take thy beak from out my heart, and take thy form from off my door!'
            Quoth the Raven 'Nevermore.'

And the Raven, never flitting, still is sitting, <u>still</u> is sitting
On the pallid bust of Pallas just above my chamber door;
And his eyes have all the seeming of a demon's that is dreaming,
And the lamp-light o'er him streaming throws his shadow on the floor;
And my soul from out that shadow that lies floating on the floor
            Shall be lifted – nevermore!

EDGAR ALLAN POE

AFTER READING

1 What is the basic storyline of Poe's tale? Retell it in between three and five simple statements.

2 What does the Raven mean when he says 'Nevermore'?

3 How is rhyme used in this poem?

British Prime Minister Winston Churchill also turned his hand to writing fiction. This little-known short story shows how he builds suspense.

'Man Overboard!'

It was a little after half-past nine when the man fell overboard. The mail steamer was hurrying through the Red Sea in the hope of making up the time which the currents of the Indian Ocean had stolen. The night was clear, though the moon was hidden behind clouds. The warm air was laden with moisture. The still surface of the waters was only broken by the movement of the great ship, from whose quarter the long, slanting undulations struck out, like the feathers from an arrow shaft, and in whose wake the froth and air bubbles churned up by the propeller trailed in a narrowing line to the darkness of the horizon.

There was a concert on board. All the passengers were glad to break the monotony of the voyage, and gathered around the piano in the companion-house. The decks were deserted. The man had been listening to the music and joining in the songs. But the room was hot, and he came out to smoke a cigarette and enjoy a breath of the wind which the speedy passage of the liner created. It was the only wind in the Red Sea that night.

The accommodation-ladder had not been unshipped since leaving Aden, and the man walked out on to the platform, as on to a balcony. He leaned his back against the rail and blew a puff of smoke into the air reflectively. The piano struck up a lively turn, and a voice began to sing the first verse of 'The Rowdy Dowdy Boys'. The measured pulsations of the screw were a subdued but additional accompaniment. The man knew the song. It had been the rage at all the music halls, when he had started for India seven years before. It reminded him of the brilliant and busy streets he had not seen for so long, but was soon to see again. He was just going to join in the chorus, when the railing, which had been insecurely fastened, gave way suddenly with a snap, and he fell backwards into the warm water of the sea amid a great splash.

For a moment he was physically too much astonished to think. Then he realized that he must shout. He began to do this even before he rose to the surface. He achieved a hoarse, inarticulate, half-choked scream. A startled brain suggested the word 'Help!' and he bawled this out lustily and with frantic effort six or seven times without stopping. Then he listened.

> *Hi! hi! clear the way*
> *For the Rowdy Dowdy Boys.*

The chorus floated back to him across the smooth water, for the ship had already passed completely by. And as he heard the music a long stab of terror drove through his heart. The possibility that he would not be picked up dawned for the first time on his consciousness. The chorus started again –

> *Then–I–say–boys,*
> *Who's for a jolly spree?*
> *Rum–tum–tiddley–um,*
> *Who'll have a drink with me?*

'Help! help! help!' shrieked the man, in desperate fear.

> *Fond of a glass now and then,*
> *Fond of a row or noise;*
> *Hi! hi! clear the way*
> *For the Rowdy Dowdy Boys!*

The last words drawled out faint and fainter. The vessel was steaming fast. The beginning of the second verse was confused and broken by ever-growing distance. The dark outline of the great hull was getting blurred. The stern light dwindled.

Then he set out to swim after it with furious energy, pausing every dozen strokes to shout long wild shouts. The disturbed waters of the sea began to settle again to their rest. The widening undulations became ripples. The aerated confusion of the screw fizzed itself upwards and out. The noise of motion and the sounds of life and music died away.

The liner was but a single fading light on the blackness of the waters and a dark shadow against the paler sky.

At length full realization came to the man, and he stopped swimming. He was alone – abandoned. With the understanding his brain reeled. He began again to swim, only now instead of shouting he prayed – mad, incoherent prayers, the words stumbling into one another.

Suddenly a distant light seemed to flicker and brighten.

A surge of joy and hope rushed through his mind. They were going to stop – to turn the ship and come back. And with the hope came gratitude. His prayer was answered. Broken words of thanksgiving rose to his lips. He stopped and stared after the light – his soul in his eyes. As he watched it, it grew gradually but steadily smaller. Then the man knew that his fate was certain. Despair succeeded hope. Gratitude gave place to curses. Beating the water with his arms, he raved impotently. Foul oaths burst from him, as broken as his prayers – and as unheeded.

The fit of passion passed, hurried by increasing fatigue. He became silent – silent as was the sea, for even the ripples were subsiding into the glassy smoothness of the surface. He swam on mechanically along the track of the ship, sobbing quietly to himself, in the misery of fear. And the stern light became a tiny speck, yellowed but scarcely bigger than some of the stars, which here and there shone between the clouds.

Nearly twenty minutes passed, and the man's fatigue began to change to exhaustion. The overpowering sense of the inevitable pressed upon him. With the weariness came a strange comfort. He need not swim all the long way to Suez. There was another course. He would die. He would resign his existence since he was thus abandoned. He threw up his hands impulsively and sank. Down, down he went through the warm water. The physical death took hold of him and he began to drown. The pain of the savage grip recalled his anger. He fought with it furiously. Striking out with arms and legs he sought to get back to the air. it was a hard struggle, but he escaped victorious and gasping to the surface. Despair awaited him. Feebly splashing with his hands he moaned in bitter misery –

'I can't – I must. O God! Let me die.'

The moon, then in her third quarter, pushed out from behind the concealing clouds and shed a pale, soft glitter upon the sea. Upright in the water, fifty yards away, was a black triangular object. It was a fin. It approached him slowly.

His last appeal had been heard.

WINSTON CHURCHILL

1 How was the outcome of the story different from what you expected?

2 Why do you think the writer keeps including lyrics from the song in his story?

COMPARE

Discussion

1   Working in a small group, design a graph so that a reader can compare the three stories visually. Among other things, your graph should show:

- which story is most/least horrifying
- which creates most/least suspense
- which contains the most/least complex language.

2   Discuss the way in which the different stories are told, using these questions as your starting points:

- How does the narrator in each story differ?
- How can you tell from the language that the stories were written long ago? Which story do you think is the oldest?
- In what ways does the use of verse affect the tone of 'The Raven' in comparison to the other two stories?

Assignments

1   Write a personal response to the three stories, describing

- what you like or dislike about them
- which elements create fear or suspense
- which parts feel too dated to work these days
- how difficult they were to understand.

2   As an experiment, take Winston Churchill's story and rewrite it in verse. You might start by comparing it with William Cowper's eighteenth-century poem 'The Castaway' – also about a man overboard – to get some ideas about verse form and style. Or try and imitate the style of other poems you have read.

Then write a paragraph explaining what you have written and commenting on its effect: what has been gained and lost from the original story?

3   Why has our fascination with the story of *Frankenstein* continued over 200 years? Compare the presentation of Dr Frankenstein and his monster with a film version.

WRITING HORROR

■ Writer Tim Crawley was given a challenge similar to that which led Mary Shelley to write *Frankenstein.* He was asked to write a short horror story which contained an ordinary object as a central element. In his accompanying essay, Tim Crawley explains how he responded to the challenge and created *Cold Hands.*

READING SKILLS
Summarising
Analysing language
Developing personal response

Cold Hands

It was too dark to see the picture, although there was a faint white smudge in the darkness which it could have been. Lucy increased her pace and a fluttering built up somewhere between her chest and her stomach. She had left junior school years ago, but for some reason that picture was still there, stuck up in the window of her old classroom. She didn't like to think about it, that picture in red crayon of a smiling boy with outstretched arms. The smile looked painful, desperate. She didn't like to think about it, or about who had drawn it.

She cleared her throat to make a noise, and bit her tongue severely. She thought she could smell the rust on the railings but then realized she was tasting her own blood. What was the matter with her? She was normally calmer than this.

As if she expected it, on the last spike of the railing fence, as if it was hitching a lift, was impaled a child's red woollen mitten. In that fading light, with its pattern of white reindeer on red wool, the glove looked impossibly small, and something in her snapped, something which had been threatening to go for a long time. She found herself sobbing as if someone she loved had died. She put one hand onto the railings to steady herself, and completely abandoned herself to the pain that flowed through her. Something was stirring in her memory, something she did not want to think about.

After a while she became aware of a softness against her face. She froze, then realized it was her own hand holding the glove from the fence. The wool caught on the Velcro on her coat collar. Ripping it away released a smell of damp wool and the talcum-powdery tang of a small child.

'Someone's going to have a cold hand,' she breathed to herself. At that moment there was a thin cry, like a child's shout at play and the sound of toddling feet came towards her. She turned with a smile.

A small black and white cat crossed the road, and a place passed overhead with its navigation lights flashing. A man who had been clipping his hedge, moving his nose closer to the blades as the light faded, finally gave up. A streetlight flickered from dull red to orange. Other than that, the road was empty. She turned again to see if the child had passed her.

Nothing.

Suddenly she was running, and she didn't care who saw her run or what they thought.

Without thinking, she had put the glove in her pocket.

Sadly for Lucy, her mother was in one of her 'I must show an interest in my daughter' moods. Lucy was feeling pretty foolish about her earlier panic and didn't want to be spoken to until she had come to terms with it.

'So what did you do at school today? Anything good?'

'Not really.' Lucy tried to side-step her beaming mother and scoot up to her room, but her mother moved in front of her.

'Is that it? This is your exam year and that's all you can say?'

'Yes!' Her irritation with her mother made her forget for a moment the sound of small feet scampering in an empty street.

'I think one of your posters has fallen off the wall again, or one of your piles of magazines has fallen over, because I heard some noises coming from in there. I thought you had sneaked in. I didn't go in because you know I don't venture in without an armed escort, ha ha, in case a coffee cup bites me, ha ha....Lucy!' Lucy barged past her mother, blood pounding in her ears. Her mother shook her head and retired sadly to the kitchen.

Once Lucy reached the door to her room she suddenly lost the will to act. Her mother was probably right. What else could the noise have been? Nevertheless she found herself putting an ear to the cold painted wood, and waiting until her heart stopped thudding enough for her to listen.

Nothing. She cautiously opened the door. Everything was in place. It looked like chaos but she knew its every detail. All the posters were in place and the piles of clothes, books and magazines were leaning but intact. Perhaps it was one of her mother's little jokes. She turned to look at her face and hair in the mirror on her dressing table.

Underneath the picture of her latest least favourite group, on which she had drawn silly noses and other things, was some writing in lipstick. There was the word 'Mine!' and underneath a shaky drawing of a mitten, more like a signature than anything else. She couldn't believe it and she bent closer to look. It wasn't lipstick; it was a reddish brown colour, one that wouldn't go at all with her yellowish complexion. A smell in the room told her what it was: wax crayon, the smell that almost conjured up a whole primary classroom for her. She smiled, remembering, then stopped smiling. She had no crayons, and who had written it? She heard a breathing shadowing her own. She stopped and it did too. She laughed nervously and a laughter shadowed hers and didn't quite stop when she did.

Lucy couldn't believe how everything had changed. Her lovely, friendly, messy room now had too many dark corners and shadows. She knew she wouldn't be able to stay there until every corner of it had been cleared, satisfying herself that she was alone. She didn't know how that writing had got there. She didn't want to know. She knew that the things she was imagining couldn't be true.

She had soon filled two black bin bags with rubbish and collected a tray full of dirty mugs. She ignored her mother's bemused look when she asked for a duster and polish.

The wax crayon was hard to remove because it has

been pressed on so hard. It was a boy, she thought, one who pressed hard like...then she blotted out the thought.

When finished, it looked as tidy as a hotel room. She had found nothing unusual and she felt pretty silly. Only the writing on the mirror was singular in its oddness. It was now gone from the glass, if not from her mind.

Feeling easier in herself she went down to eat, and then, unusually, spent the whole evening watching television with her parents instead of on her own set in her room. Her father made life slightly uncomfortable, as usual, by making what he thought were very funny remarks about her.

When he changed the channel from a good violent film to *Question Time*, she said goodnight.

'Thanks for popping in, Your Majesty! See you again one day?' Her father put out a hand for her to shake.

She lay on her bed and wondered why it was her father could wind her up so much. She wished she could hate him and not care if he was unkind to her. She closed her eyes and hugged her pillow to her chest.

The sun shone yellow beams into the high bright room. She was sitting at a low table as the sound of children playing roared outside, a high voice repeating, 'You're it! You're it! You're it!' Her hands were smaller and chubbier than normal. 'I'm a little girl!' she shrieked laughing. She had some pinkish plasticine on the table in front of her and she noticed that her hands were making a model boy. It had nostrils and eye-lashes and hair. It looked asleep. Somebody was standing behind her, she could hear him breathing.

'Leave me alone,' she whispered. The breathing moved closer to her neck until she could feel it. She smoothed the forehead of the figure lying on the table. A whistle blew outside and other children came into the room talking and laughing. They crowded round her table. 'That's good,' they all said. 'It's just like he was.'

'Like who?' She looked at the figure more closely. It was true, it did look familiar. As her breath fell onto it, the tiny eyes sprang open and the figure began to writhe, its mouth opening as if it was in terrible pain.

The creature was tearing at its sides in agony. Her heart was breaking for it and her hands began to tear the figure into pieces to stop the suffering as quickly as possible but the individual pieces continued to writhe.

'Look what you've done!' The children pointed not at the figure on the table but at the one behind her.

She turned her head whimpering, not wanting to see.

A misshapen figure of bone and blood leapt down to her. It shot out a hand and grabbed hers and squeezed so hard, her bones crunched. 'Mine!' it bubbled through its torn lips. She screamed...

... and screamed awake, throwing the pillow away from her. Her hand for a moment retained the pressure of a bony grip. She fought for breath and got it in whooping gusts.

She flinched and the light came on and backed away as a large figure blundered towards her. She batted away hands that reached for her and then weakly collapsed into them recognising her mother.

'Oh horrible!'

'Shhh! It was just a dream. Come on, get changed for bed properly, you're soaked with sweat.' Her mother looked dumbfounded around the room. 'Well! What a good job you've done. What polish did you use? Smells just like plasticine.'

Her mother's chilling words made sure she didn't sleep again that night, but, just as the sun rose, she must have nodded off. She felt herself smile as her mother gently stroked her face.

She awoke with a name in her mind, Ross Dermott. The room was blasted with sunlight and her door was closed. Her mother had obviously left while she was sleeping although she could still feel the warmth of her hand against her cheek.

There was something wrong with the light, and Lucy looked at her clock.

'Oh my God!' she leapt up and ran to her door. 'Mum, it's quarter to ten!'

'It's OK, I phoned school for you. I thought you

needed a day off after last night.' Her mother's voice had a strange echoing quality as it bounced up the stairs. Lucy flopped back on the bed and closed her eyes, half relieved, half uneasy. The name Ross Dermott rose up again in her mind. That was who the plasticine model had reminded her of. She half laughed, then her laugh turned sour in her mouth. Ross, the scarecrow. Ross, the one who smelt of stale clothes and frying. Ross, the one who they all said had fleas and ran from at playtime. Ross, the one who cried every time his mother left him at the school gates. Ross, the one who cried when his mother never came to collect him at the end of one school day, and whom he never saw again. Ross, the one whose gloves were stolen and thrown high into bushes where he couldn't reach. And Ross...

Her mind shied away from this final thing but it was like a boomerang, the harder and further she threw it, the harder and faster it came back to hit her. Ross, the gentle, sweet and funny boy who had made her laugh and had given her a real gold ring on her birthday because he said he liked her. He said to keep it carefully because it had belonged to his mother. The ring she had dropped down a drain in front of him, while Caroline laughed, because she had been embarrassed by his gesture and couldn't handle it.

The same Ross who had been crushed to death by a JCB, on a building site while lying in some sand. A teacher had lost her job because of this. He should have been in school but he had run out at lunchtime and no one had bothered to look for him, probably because they hadn't noticed he had gone.

Lucy knew why he had run away. She was going to tell him that she had got the ring out of the drain as soon as she could. She even wore it, to show him, on the way home.

By then, of course he was dead and he would never know how she had really felt. She had kept the ring carefully in her drawer and had never discussed it, or Ross, with anyone since.

She was even convinced that she hadn't thought about him since. She knew how much effort it had cost her not to. She also remembered why the picture, in her old school window, had been left. It had been painted by Ross and, by his standards, was a work of genius. He had been so pleased to get a gold star for it. When they had tidied up at the end of the year no one had had the heart to tear up Ross's picture, but nobody had wanted to keep it either.

It was only at this moment, that Lucy admitted to herself that the picture which had frightened her so much was Ross's. Even when he had first finished it, she hadn't liked its expression. It looked in pain.

She began to cry. For the first time she realized what she had done. Red hot tracks scoured her cheeks and she felt her whole life shrink to one vicious, hilarious, evil moment. She felt too young to have to feel this huge regret.

She hadn't realized she had been crying aloud but clearly she had because her mother was stroking her face again, her cool fingers tracing her tears.

'Thanks, Mum.'

Lucy expected her mother in her normal caring but insensitive way to ask what was wrong. But she silently continued to stroke her face.

Her mother's fingers were cold and began to increase their pressure.

'Thanks, Mum.' Lucy said in the voice she reserved to express the opposite. The fingers continued to patrol her cheek, increasing pressure until they began to graze her. She was about to complain, when she clearly heard her mother singing downstairs.

Her eyes snapped open. For a moment she saw outlined against the window a figure of bone and blood and smiling eyes holding a hand towards her, fingers outspread.

'Mine!' it whispered, 'For me!' The figure leaned forward towards her, glistening.

What made her faint was the fact she could see the sun shining through its teeth. From behind.

Something warm and wet touched her face and she inhaled in order to scream.

'Shhh! The doctor's coming. I'm getting the worst of the blood off your face.'

'Blood!'

'Shhh! Shhh! Funny, I can't seem to see where it

comes from. There's some on your hand too.'

'My hand?' Lucy at that moment became aware of a tight, throbbing sensation on her left hand.

'Silly girl, you've jammed on a ring that's far too small for you. We'll have to get it cut off, your finger's all swollen up. It's on your wedding finger too! Is there something you haven't told us?' Her mother wrung out the cloth into a bowl. 'There is something you haven't told us isn't there? You're not in trouble are you?'

Lucy thought about the words the figure had spoken.

'Yes, Mum,' she said quietly, 'I'm afraid I am.'

TIM CRAWLEY

THE WRITING OF 'COLD HANDS'

*F*or me, the biggest challenge in writing *Cold Hands* was to make the central character a sympathetic, real, living person. I didn't want to invent her just to be killed or tortured; I wanted a person to care about. I also wanted there to be an atmosphere, a sense of place and time. I wanted there to be an interesting plot and, dare I say it, a moral. I only had three thousand words to play with. It sounds a lot, but it isn't.

I also have this belief that good horror fiction starts very much in the ordinary world. A football left in a gutter that looks like a head for a moment, a Guy Fawkes that appears to watch you as you walk past, or the cupboard door that swings slowly open in your room at night: all are far more disturbing than the twelve-headed purple people-eater. Horror creeps softly out of the feeling that ordinary things are not doing what they should, that commonplace events have some other logic or purpose.

So, with *Cold Hands* I started with the image of the child's mitten on the fence. Whenever I see children's lost gloves or toys, I am always moved. I always wonder if the child is missing them or why they have never come to

AFTER READING

1 The story is written in five sections. Summarise each in one sentence.

2 How is the ending of the story similar to and different from what you anticipated?

■ In this essay Tim Crawley explains how he came to write *Cold Hands*.

look for them. Gloves are particularly poignant because they are half of a pair and therefore the one left with the owner is useless and alone. The fact that the glove in the story is impaled is a deliberate running together of a harsh image with a soft vulnerable one, which I hope contributes to the atmosphere of unease.

This was my starting point, and I needed a character for this event to involve. As I said, for me the most important part is the main character, Lucy, otherwise this would be an 'empty' story. In my first draft, I let this requirement hijack my story writing. The first six hundred words or so were dedicated to describing Lucy's state of mind, and the actual story-telling was left on hold. This was pointed out by a group of Year 10 students who read and responded to the first draft. I could easily have lost a lot of readers there, so this part of the draft was axed. it wasn't a waste of time writing it though, because it gave me, as the writer, the chance to write my way into the character and the story.

I wanted a central character who was basically a good person but didn't always do the right thing and didn't always admit past wrongs she had done – a lot like most of us really. I wanted a character who felt things deeply, but was too cool to admit it. I also chose a female character for the simple reason that there are still not enough central female characters in fiction.

Having established a believable character, and related her to my original image of the lost, impaled glove, I needed a whole story or a plot. This is how I normally go about plotting. I think of a character in a certain place or in relation to a certain image and then work from there. Some writers start with a whole plot first then invent places and characters. There is no right way to do this.

My plot is a fairly traditional one, of betrayal and revenge, but I feel the motivation of the characters and the open ending gives the story more impact. Maybe Lucy, having admitted her guilt to herself, and grieving for Ross, will be forgiven. Maybe having 'claimed' him by rescuing the glove, she is destined to join him, or to be accompanied by him for the rest of her life. There could be other interpretations – that's up to you.

Readers of the first version of the story picked up what

they thought was an inconsistency in the plot, that is, the existence of both a glove and a ring. They felt, I think, that there should be only one of these things. I think they saw these items in a different way from me. I saw them as the possessions of a character we had yet to meet – Ross's way of letting Lucy know he was still around. The readers, I suspect, saw these items as the more traditional 'magic tokens', e.g. a haunted mirror. I can understand their point of view, but I stuck to mine. Both items survive to the final draft, although with an attempt by me – 'Ross, the one whose gloves were stolen and thrown high into bushes where he couldn't reach' – to make the glove more central.

Having a plot and a character, the story needed a sense of place, time and atmosphere. Once again there was some severe cutting done in this area. In the original draft there was a detailed description of an old abandoned school, where Ross's picture was supposed to hang. This had the double fault of being both totally clichéd and unconvincing. In the final draft, it has been changed to an existing school, barely described. The fact that the picture is still in the window is justified by adding that people might feel removing the work of a dead pupil was disrespectful or unlucky.

The opening scenes are set at twilight, which I think is more worrying than night-time because some things are still clearly visible, but there are lots of shadows. It is light rubbing up against dark and, metaphorically, certainty being overwhelmed by uncertainty. I use a lot of particularly ordinary images at the point Lucy hears the child: 'A small black and white cat crossed the road, and a plane passed overhead with its navigation lights flashing,' etc, to emphasise the concreteness of the world and to contrast with her sudden uncertainty and fear.

Horror writing is difficult in this regard, because a lot of the events in it are unlikely. Therefore, the writer must set the events firmly in the here and now, and hint at the unbelievable. This is what I have tried to do. The child is just an ordinary sound in an ordinary street. Ross is just a stroke on the cheek, until he is seen. Even when he is seen, – 'For a moment she saw outlined against the window a figure of bone and blood and smiling eyes

1 What have you learnt from Tim Crawley's essay which adds to your understanding or enjoyment of the story?

2 Are there any questions which he leaves unanswered?

holding a hand towards her, fingers outspread' – it is brief, concrete and simple.

Another way I tried to move the plot forward and generate an atmosphere, was to give Lucy a nightmare. This is a common device in fiction. In this case, it was used more specifically than just to promote unease. I used it to allow Lucy to remember what she had done. It is a prompt to her memory: she remembers Ross on wakening. Therefore it does some explanatory work, increases the tension and allows Lucy to remember something she has suppressed for a long time.

Overall, I feel that this story works. More than that, I feel I have, largely, achieved my aim: a horror story that does not devalue people, and doesn't preach, but does create one or two shivers. It is not perfect, and probably doesn't warrant this level of analysis, but I hope you enjoyed it.

TIM CRAWLEY

COMPARE

Discussion

1   Look back at each one of the five sections of the story and decide:

- what part each section plays in the overall story
- how much suspense there is on a scale of 1 (least) to 5 (most) in each section.

2   In his essay, Tim Crawley says that he made his main character a girl 'for the simple reason that there are still not enough central female characters in fiction'. Discuss this idea, and then discuss the way Lucy is presented: what is her character like?

3   After reading his first draft of the story, a group of Year 10 pupils gave feedback to Tim Crawley on what they liked and disliked about the story. What would your feedback be on this final version of the story?

Assignments

1   Write your own horror story using one of these ideas as a starting point:

- an empty warehouse
- a faded flower in a window
- an abandoned shop
- an old typewriter.

Then, like Tim Crawley, write a commentary on your work.

2   Write a new version of *Cold Hands* from the point of view of Lucy's mother. When did she first sense something was wrong with her daughter? How would she describe the final scene?

FILMING HORROR

■ Horror films gain much of their effect from the skills of the make-up artists who create the monster at the heart of the film. In this article journalist Calum Watson and special-effects creator Mike Moustafi describe the process of creating terrifying make-up effects.

READING SKILLS

Seeking information

Summarising

INSTANT HORROR

Special effects are widely used in films and television to create a terrifying range of illusions.

*F*EW of us would recognise Freddy Krueger without his make-up. The actor Robert Englund, who terrified audiences in the *Nightmare on Elm Street* movies, owes his appearance to the skills and innovation of specialist make-up artists.

A script writer or film director might have the original idea for a "monster" or an "alien". But it is the specialist make-up artist who must transform that vision into the reality you see on screen. The artist must combine great ingenuity and a detailed knowledge of sculpture, painting, casting and mechanical techniques to create the finished illusion.

Ageing

A FILM script may require characters to look much older than the actors playing the role.

The wrinkled texture of old skin is created using a translucent (semi-transparent) rubbery substance such as gelatine or liquid latex. The skin of the actor is stretched taut while several layers of latex are brushed on. When these layers dry and the skin tension is released, the latex will form folds and wrinkles that appear convincing.

This technique, however, cannot create the changes in the shape of a face – such as sagging cheeks and chin – that occur as we grow older. Often, the transformation of an actor into an old person or a "monster" requires a physical re-shaping technique known as "prosthetics".

Prosthetics

IN PROSTHETICS, a three-dimensional change is created in an actor's features using materials such as foam latex or moulded plastic.

Unlike its liquid counterpart, foam latex is spongy and thick. When glued to an actor's face using spirit gum or medical adhesive, and blended in with conventional make-up, it appears as an extra layer of skin.

The new "skin" allows free movement and expression both inside and outside. It can be attached to the skin either in the form of appliances such as false noses or chins or, if necessary, as a complete mask or body suit.

When prosthetics is used to re-model an actor's face, the process begins with many hours of preplanning and sketching. Often a very detailed cast of the actor's head and shoulders is taken using a moulding compound such as Alginate. The Alginate dries quickly, producing a cast that is so detailed that it even picks up the pores of the skin.

This cast is then used to create a replica of the actor's head and shoulders. The replica serves as a model for the make-up specialist to work on. It is built up with clay and carefully sculpted into the desired final appearance.

Finally, a second cast of the finished sculpture is taken. This can be used to create a perfectly fitting latex mask.

Animatronics

A PROSTHETIC mask can become so built up that it loses the ability to convey the physical expressions of the actor beneath it. In such cases "animatronic" techniques are used to control expression and movement mechanically.

Inside the mask the foam latex is typically supported by a fibreglass underskull or "armature". This fulfils much the same role as a human skeleton.

A variety of mechanisms such as cables, electric servo (radiohope controlled) motors and inflatable rubber bladders are used in place of muscles. These are then operated to manipulate the mask so that its lip or eyebrow movements are convincing.

Make-up effects

IN FILMS, an "effect" is literally an event that must be seen to happen in front of the camera. An example of a common make-up effect is when a script requires an actor to be seen receiving a gunshot wound.

One way of achieving this is to attach small smokeless explosive charges known as "squibs" to the actor's skin. These are mounted on steel plates to protect the actor and can be surrounded by small bags of stage blood. Once attached to an actor's skin, they can be blended into the skin using foam latex. They can be electrically detonated during filming.

Prosthetic moulding techniques and animatronics are often combined to create apparently impossible effects. At crucial stages of filming a false limb or even a full-size replica of the actor can be substituted to create an impressive illusion.

The results achieved by professional make-up artists involve specialist equipment and expensive materials. But you can create your own simple make-up illusions using everyday materials (see illustrations below).

Monster mask

You will need strips of reinforced plaster (such as Modroc, which you can buy in model shops), petroleum jelly (such as Vaseline), cling film and a bowl of warm water. You will also need a "model". **An adult should be present.**

Carefully coat your model's face, particularly the eyebrows and the hairline, with petroleum jelly. Use cling film to cover the hair, but **never** the face. Cut the reinforced plaster into 3cm-wide strips.

Dip a strip into the water to soften the plaster. Squeeze out excess water through two fingers. Apply it to your model's face, starting with the forehead. Apply further strips, each one slightly overlapping a previous one. Leave the eyes and nostrils uncovered. Build up the mask until it is three layers deep.

Carefully remove the mask and fasten some strips of cloth to the edges to attach it to the wearer's head. After hardening overnight, the mask can be built up further using more plaster, rose thorns, hairs, paint, etc, to create your finished "monster".

Hair covered in cling film →

Modroc built up in layers →

THE GUARDIAN

1 Skim through the extract again and find answers to these questions:

- What does prosthetics mean?
- What is animatronics?
- What is an armature?
- What are squibs?
- What is Modroc?

Discussion

1 What have you learnt from reading the article? What questions do you have which the article did not answer?

2 What age of readership is the article aimed at? How can you tell?

3 How clear and how practical are the instructions given on making a monster mask? How could they be improved?

Use the four headings – *Ageing*, *Prosthetics*, *Animatronics* and *Make-up effects*. For each one think of one sentence to summarise the information given.

Assignments

1 How would you rewrite this article in simpler language for a younger audience, e.g. eight year olds? How would you explain some of the difficult technical words? Write a 200-word version of it, simplifying and clarifying its main ideas.

2 Think of a process you are familiar with – such as mending a puncture or making a telephone call from a phone box. Write a set of clear instructions, including illustrations if necessary, as if addressing someone who has never seen the process before.

3 Make a study of special-effects techniques in some television programmes or films. Write an analysis of what they add to the story's overall effect. Are there some programmes/films you can think of in which the effects are stunning, but the basic storyline and characterisation poor?

WIDER READING

Horror fiction
Kurt Singer (ed), *The First Target Book of Horror* and *The Second Target Book of Horror*; Julian Lloyd Webber (ed), *Short Sharp Shocks*; J N Williamson (ed), *Flesh Creepers*; Edgar Allan Poe, *Selected Stories*; Robert Westall (ed), *Ghost Stories*.

Non-fiction
Daniel Farson, *The Hamlyn Book of Horror*; Aiden Chambers, *Great British Ghosts*; Reader's Digest, *Mysteries of the Unexplained*.

AFTER READING

1 Write a list of essential horror-story ingredients, then compare two stories from your reading in terms of their characterisation and their creation of suspense and fear.

2 Write a personal essay about people's fascination with horror stories. Illustrate it with examples from your own reading.

CHARACTER BUILDING

In books, as in life, we encounter a huge variety of characters. What ingredients do authors use to create believable and interesting people? How are our own characters formed? Are we born with certain features of personality already in place, or do we acquire them from our parents and friends?

- *Think about the way you are seen by other people.*
- *Compare some characters from real-life and fiction.*

THE PRICE OF FAME

■ Should famous people's characters be open for constant examination in the media? Compare the following three extracts.

READING SKILLS
Summarising
Studying genre
Distinguishing fact from fiction/detecting bias

AFTER READING

1 Do you know any facts about Michael Jackson which you think are missing from this biography?

2 Are there any statements in the extract which are opinion rather than fact?

A DICTIONARY OF TWENTIETH CENTURY WORLD BIOGRAPHY, 1992

Jackson, Michael (1958 –   )
US singer and songwriter, who became the top-selling pop artist of the 1980s.

Born in Gary, Indiana, he was the youngest of the original Jackson Five, a successful black pop group of the 1970s consisting of the five (later six) Jackson brothers. He sang on most of the group's recordings but released songs under his own name as early as 1971 when 'Got to Be There' became a major hit. However, his full-time solo career did not start until 1979, when *Off the Wall* became the bestselling album by a black artist to date; it included songs written by Paul McCartney as well as songs by Jackson himself. The up-tempo album *Thriller* (1983) was even more successful and Jackson's skill as a dancer was exploited to the full in spectacular accompanying videos. Songs from the album and its successor, *Bad* (1987), confirmed Jackson's status as the most commercial US star of the decade. The success of the albums and videos was further enhanced by a plethora of stories about Jackson's reclusive lifestyle, especially such eccentricities as his exotic pets, extreme vegetarianism, and rumoured cosmetic surgery.

'Planet Earth, gentle and blue,
With all my heart, I love you.'

Michael Jackson comes to Britain next week.
Catherine Bennett went to Stockholm to see what the
worshippers are waiting for.

A glance in Michael's mirror

WHO SAID this? "I wanted to change the world. So I got up one morning and looked in the mirror." God? The Yorkshire Ripper? No. Michael Jackson. And what did Michael see when he looked in the mirror? A wet-look kiss-curl, a lot of eyeliner, and that funny little nose modelled on the snout of a hedgehog? No.

Jackson saw pain. Pain, globally. "A child crying in Ethiopia, a seagull struggling pathetically in an oil spill, a mountain gorilla being mercilessly hunted, a teenage soldier trembling with terror when he hears the planes fly over." And he had a God-like reaction to these traumas. "Aren't these things happening in *me* when I see and hear about them?"

Well, no, they're not. Michael Jackson not being God, merely an American singing and dancing act of passably anthropoid appearance, these things aren't actually happening in him when he sees and hears about them. That's a lot of twaddle. But it's the thought that counts, eh? Particularly to Michael Jackson's fans.

"He brings joy," exclaims a girl called Camilla, one of a crowd waiting at midnight outside Michael Jackson's hotel on the Stockholm stop of his current European tour, chanting "Mike-*uhl*, Mike-*uhl*", and caterwauling "Uh, *uh; uh, uh; Billy Jean is *not* my lovah!" "I think he's a great personality," Camilla says, keeping a weather eye on the hotel facade, lest Jackson's sequined glove should come stealing out in benediction from behind a net curtain, "because he's not thinking about himself, just about children and the world, and about the planet earth, which he adores." Indeed he does. He says so in his new poetry book which Camilla bought at the concert: "Planet Earth, gentle and blue/With all my heart, I love you." There.

Other ditties and "reflections" attest to Jackson's love of dolphins, squirrels, furry baby seals, big sad elephants, angels, mother ("No matter where I go from here/You're in my heart, my mother dear") and babies ("In the garden/We frolic awhile/Those are moments when babies smile.") but there are no angels on the street in Stockholm. There are just clusters of adolescent girls, wearing damp anoraks, shrieking His praise.

Pearl? Furl? Twirl? Churl? It's true that the world girl doesn't rhyme with much, but that doesn't altogether explain Jackson leaving girls out of all the poems about his favourite things. God only rhymes with unprepossessing words like bod, sod, cod and tod, but Michael managed to work up a reflection on *Him*. Couldn't he have included just one reflection on girls, as a gesture towards the bedraggled creatures who mope outside hotel lobbies in all weathers, reaching out with roses and letters, their only reward a security man's armlock?

But maybe Jackson thought he's said all there was to say about girls in this crowd scene from his biography, Moonwalk: "Those girls were *serious*. They still are... One girl is twisting your wrist this way while another girl is pulling your watch off...Early on, I learned how to run through crowds of thrashing girls outside of theatres, hotels and airports. It's important to remember to shield your eyes with your hands because girls can forget they have nails during such emotional confrontations." The most emotional confrontation, he adds, took place in Britain.

"I *had* to touch him," says Amanda Woolley, shortly to rename herself Amanda Jackson, a Michael Jackson votary who once spent six months writing half a million pleases in a fruitless bid for an audience. When Jackson last visited London, Amanda wept on the shop floor of Harrods until her employers gave her leave to wait with the other fans outside the Dorchester.

When Jackson returned from shopping, there occurred what Amanda, a delicate-looking girl, nicely describes as a "kerfuffle", which allowed her to slink, not unnoticed, into the lobby. "Security were saying get out, get out, and I was like, clinging in with my nails, and saying, I just have to see him."

Jackson passed by pressed almost to the ground by the tonnage of girls. "We got into a crush, and I stroked his back and I said, 'Are you okay? I love you', so it was like, well worth it." Amanda looks a little bashful. "Some people would say, how come you didn't like kiss and grapple him, but I say no, I was genuinely concerned that he was getting crushed. He said 'Yeah, I'm okay', he like bent up, he acknowledged me – then I came out."

So far as it is known, Jackson's emotional history suggests that a llama, a personable rat or even a seagull struggling pathetically in an oil spill, would stand a better chance of sharing his amusement park for better for worse, for richer for poorer, in sickness and in health. Some fans, such as Camilla of Stockholm, have learnt this hard lesson. Less than half Jackson's age, she wants to mother, not seduce or marry him; to be Wendy to his Peter Pan. J M Barrie's Wendy is intensely interested when Peter says, "I don't want to grow up ever!...I don't want to be a man. I want to stay a little boy

and have fun. That's why I ran away and lived with the fairies in Kensington Gardens.

And when Jackson, who lives with llamas in Neverland, California, pretends to blub on stage, Camilla is equally stirred. "You just want to give him a hug and a kiss and tell him, 'Oh, it's all right Michael, you're very good. He seems like a child, he seems so innocent."

But isn't it more queer than touching, this 33-year-old man wanting to be like a child? "I think it's his childhood," Camilla explains, maternally, "Because he never had the chance to be a child when he was a child. It's not easy for him to make friends. That's Michael."

THE GUARDIAN

1 Summarise the main facts of the article.

2 Choose a word which you think best describes the writer's attitude to Michael Jackson.

Nancy Reagan

THE UNAUTHORIZED BIOGRAPHY

*T*wo entries on Nancy Reagan's birth certificate are accurate – her sex and her colour. Almost every other item has been revised. In truth, the certificate itself gave birth to two generations of lies.

The original facts about the infant Anne Frances Robbins, now Nancy Reagan, were carefully rewritten.

She revised her date of birth, concealed her birthplace, and cast aside her father.

In her memoirs, she asserted she forgot the name of the hospital where she was born and added that 'it burned down years ago'. In fact, not only did Sloane Hospital in New York City not burn down, but according to its official history it did not have a fire.

As for her date of birth, Nancy said coyly at the age of sixty-nine, 'I still haven't made up my mind'. The certificate says she was born 6 July 1921. But when she grew up, she altered the date to 1923 – thereby taking off two years.

When her mother gave her own age on her daughter's birth certificate, she took off four years; she was thirty-three at Nancy's birth. Her husband was twenty-seven, but she listed him as twenty-eight. Edith Luckett's birthplace is recorded as Petersburg, Virginia. In fact, she was born in Washington, DC. She is listed as a housewife, but she was an actress, a déclassé profession in those days.

Anne Frances Robbins fabricated not only a new background for herself, but also a new foreground. She was named for her father's great-great-great grandmother, Anne Ayres, and her maternal grandmother, Sarah Frances. The baby girl was nicknamed Nancy by her mother. At the age of seventeen, Anne Frances went to court to change her entire name. She dropped her father's name and eventually dropped him.

Her father was a 'Princeton graduate from a well-to-do family', she asserted in her memoirs. In fact, he did not attend Princeton – or any college. His family, from Pittsfield, Massachusetts, was not well-to-do. But even after disowning him Nancy clung to those pretensions.

When the brown-haired, brown-eyed Anne Frances was born, her parents were living in a poor section of Flushing, Queens, an outer borough of New York City. They were renting one floor of a two-storey frame house on Amity Street near the railroad tracks.

Nancy Reagan spent so many years redesigning the facts of her life that she came to accept her masquerade as real. By the time she became First Lady, the mask had become the face. History was about to be deceived.

'The truth is rarely pure', wrote Oscar Wilde in *The Importance of Being Earnest*, 'and never simple.' The retrieval of Nancy Reagan's birth certificate – the one tie to her past she has been unable to shed – provides the world with an opportunity to take a second look at its First Lady. A look at the face behind the mask.

KITTY KELLEY

AFTER READING

1 Summarise the main facts we learn here about Nancy Reagan

2 How would you describe the writer's attitude to Nancy Reagan?

COMPARE

Discussion

1 For each of the three extracts, discuss in pairs the ratio of facts to opinion (e.g. 50:50). Which one is most, and which least, factual?

2 Discuss which extract is:

- Most informative
- Most critical of its subject
- Most readable
- Most humorous

Give examples to support your choices.

3 Discuss this statement in the light of the extracts: 'If a writer doesn't like a celebrity's character, he or she should just ignore it instead of attacking it.' How far do you agree?

Assignments

1 From reading Kitty Kelley's account of Nancy Reagan, put together a 100-word factual account of her life, like the biography of Michael Jackson at the start of this section.

2 Find a profile of a celebrity in a newspaper or magazine, and write an analysis of the way it is written. Aim to write a paragraph, with examples from the text, on each of the points below.

- Starting-point (does the article begin with the celebrity's birth or at a significant point in his or her life?)
- Balance of fact and fiction
- Author's attitude to the celebrity
- Style (e.g. humorous, positive, critical, etc)

3 If you were Michael Jackson or Nancy Reagan, how do you think you would react to the passages written about you? Choose either Michael Jackson or Nancy Reagan and write a letter of reply from his or her point of view, referring to specific points in the newspaper article or the biography.

FATHER & SON

■ These two extracts – one from a nineteenth-century novel, the other from a modern autobiograpy – deal with the relationships between fathers and sons.

READING SKILLS

Developing personal response

Analysing language

Dombey and Son

✦ Chapter 1 ✦

Dombey sat in the corner of the darkened room in the great armchair by the bedside, and Son lay tucked up warm in a little basket bedstead, carefully disposed on a low settee immediately in front of the fire and close to it, as if his constitution were analogous to that of a muffin, and it was essential to toast him brown while he was very new.

Dombey was about eight-and-forty years of age. Son about eight-and-forty minutes. Dombey was rather bald, rather red, and though a handsome well-made man, too stern and pompous in appearance, to be prepossessing. Son was very bald, and very red, and though (of course) an undeniably fine infant, somewhat crushed and spotty in his general effect, as yet. On the brow of Dombey, Time and his brother Care had set some marks, as on a tree that was to come down in good time – remorseless twins they are for striding through their human forests, notching as they go – while the countenance of Son was crossed with a thousand little creases, which the same deceitful Time would take delight in smoothing out and wearing away with the flat part of his scythe, as a preparation of the surface for his deeper operations.

Dombey, exulting in the long-looked-for event, jingled and jingled the heavy gold watch-chain that depended from below his trim blue coat, whereof the buttons sparkled phosphorescently in the feeble rays of the distant fire. Son, with his little fists curled up and clenched, seemed, in his feeble way to be squaring at existence for having come upon him so unexpectedly.

'The House will once again, Mrs Dombey,' said Mr Dombey, 'be not only in name but in fact Dombey and Son;' and he added, in a tone of luxurious satisfaction, with his eyes half-closed as if he were reading the name in a device of flowers, and inhaling their fragrance at the same time; 'Dombey and Son!'

The words had such a softening influence, that he appended a term of endearment to Mrs Dombey's name (though not without some hesitation, as being a man but little used to that form of address): and said, 'Mrs Dombey, my – my dear.' A transient flush of faint surprise overspread the sick lady's face as she raised her eyes towards him.

'He will be christened Paul, my – Mrs Dombey – of course.'

She feebly echoed, 'Of course,' or rather expressed it by the motion of her lips, and closed her eyes again.

'His father's name, Mrs Dombey, and his grandfather's! I wish his grandfather were alive this day! There is some inconvenience in the necessity of writing Junior,' said Mr Dombey, making a fictitious autograph on his knee; 'but it is merely of a private and personal complexion. It doesn't enter into the correspondence of the House. *Its* signature remains the same.' And again he said 'Dombey and Son,' in exactly the same tone as before.

Those three words conveyed the one idea of Mr Dombey's life. The earth was made for Dombey and Son to trade in, and the sun and moon were made to give them light. Rivers and seas were formed to float their ships; rainbows gave them promise of fair weather; winds blew for or against their enterprises; stars and plants circled in their orbits, to preserve inviolate a system of which they were the centre. Common abbreviations took new meanings in his eyes, and had sole reference to them. A.D. had no concern with anno Domini, but stood for anno Dombei – and Son.

He had risen, as his father had before him, in the course of life and death, from Son to Dombey, and for nearly twenty years had been the sole representative of the Firm. Of those years he had been married, ten – married, as some said, to a lady with no heart to give him; whose happiness was in the past, and who was content to bind her broken spirit to the dutiful and meek endurance of the present. Such idle talk was little likely to reach the ears of Mr Dombey, whom it nearly concerned; and probably no one in the world would have received it with such utter incredulity as he, if it had reached him. Dombey and Son had often dealt in hides, but never in hearts. They left that fancy ware to boys and girls, and boarding-schools and books. Mr Dombey would have reasoned: That a matrimonial alliance with himself *must,* in the nature of things, be gratifying and honourable to any woman of common sense. That the hope of giving birth to a new partner in such a House, could not fail to awaken a glorious and stirring ambition in the breast of the least ambitious of her sex. That Mrs Dombey had entered on that social contract of matrimony: almost necessarily part of a genteel and wealthy station, even without reference to the perpetuation of family Firms: with her eyes fully open to these advantages. That Mrs Dombey had had daily practical knowledge of his position in society. That Mrs Dombey had always sat at the head of his table, and done the honours of his house in a remarkably lady-like and becoming manner. That Mrs Dombey must have been happy. That she couldn't help it.

Or, at all events, with one drawback. Yes. That he would have allowed. With only one; but that one certainly involving much. With the drawback of hope deferred, which, (as the Scripture very correctly tells us, Mr Dombey would have added in a patronising way; for his highest distinct idea even of Scripture, if examined, would have been found to be, that as forming part of a general whole, of which Dombey and Son formed another part, it was therefore to be commended and upheld) maketh the heart sick. They had been married ten years, and until this present day on which Mr Dombey sat jingling and jingling his heavy gold watch-chain in the great armchair by the side of the bed, had had no issue.

– To speak of; none worth mentioning. There had been a girl some six years before, and the child, who had stolen into the chamber unobserved, was now crouching timidly, in a corner whence she could see her mother's face. But what was a girl to Dombey and Son! In the capital of the House's name and dignity, such a child was merely a piece of base coin that couldn't be invested – a bad Boy – nothing more.

Mr Dombey's cup of satisfaction was so full at this moment, however, that he felt he could afford a drop or two of its contents, even to sprinkle on the dust in the by-path of his little daughter.

So he said, 'Florence, you may go and look at your pretty brother, if you like, I daresay. Don't touch him!'

The child glanced keenly at the blue coat and stiff white cravat, which, with a pair of creaking boots and a very loud ticking watch, embodied her idea of a father; but her eyes returned to her mother's face immediately, and she neither moved nor answered.

CHARLES DICKENS

AFTER READING

1 What are the similarities between Mr Dombey's appearance and that of his new-born son?

2 How would you describe Mr Dombey's attitude to his daughter Florence?

3 How can you tell that the novel was written in the nineteenth century? Find examples to support your ideas.

And when did you last see your Father?

A hot September Saturday in Cheshire, 1959. We haven't moved for ten minutes. Ahead of us, a queue of cars stretches out of sight around the corner. Everyone has turned his engine off, and now my father does so too. In the sudden silence we can hear the distant whine of what must be the first race of the afternoon, a ten-lap event for saloon cars. It is five minutes past one. In an hour the drivers will be warming up for the main event, the Gold Cup – Graham Hill, Jack Brabham, Roy Salvadori, Stirling Moss and Joakim Bonnier.

My father has always loved fast cars, and motor racing has a strong British following just now, which is why we are stuck here in this country lane with hundreds of other cars. My father does not like waiting in queues. He is used to patients waiting in queues to see him, but he is not used to waiting in queues himself. A queue to him means a man being denied the right to be where he wants to be at a time of his own choosing, which is at the front, now. Ten minutes have passed and my father is running out of patience. What is happening up ahead? What fat-head has caused this snarl-up? Why are no cars coming the other way? Has there been an accident? Why are there no police to sort it out? Every two minutes or so he gets out of the car, crosses to the opposite verge and tries to see if there is movement up ahead. There isn't. He gets back in. The roof of our Alvis is down, the sun beating on to the leather upholstery, the chrome, the picnic basket. The hood is folded and pleated into the mysterious crevice between the boot and the narrow back seat where my sister and I are scrunched together as usual. The roof is nearly always down, whatever the weather: my father loves fresh air, and every car he has ever owned has been a convertible, so that he can have fresh air. But the air today is not fresh. There is a pall of high-rev exhaust, dust, petrol, boiling-over engines.

In the cars ahead and behind, people are laughing, eating sandwiches, drinking from beer bottles, enjoying the weather, settling into the familiar indignity of waiting-to-get-to-the-front.

But my father is not like them. There are only two things on his mind: the invisible head of the queue and, not unrelated, the other half of the country lane, tantalizingly empty.

'Just relax, Arthur,' my mother says. 'You're in and out of the car like a blue-tailed fly.'

But being told to relax only incenses him. 'What can it be?' he demands. 'Maybe they're waiting for an ambulance.' We all know where this last speculation is leading, even before he says it. 'Maybe they need a doctor.'

'No, Arthur,' says my mother, as he opens the door for a final time and stands on the wheel arch to crane ahead.

'It must be an accident,' he announces. 'I think I should drive ahead and see.'

' No, Arthur. It's just the numbers waiting to get in. And surely there must be doctors on the circuit.'

It is one-thirty and silent now. The saloon race has finished. It is still an hour until the Gold Cup itself, but there's another race first, and the cars in the paddock to see, and besides...

'Well, I'm not going to bloody well wait here any longer,' he says. 'We'll never get in. We might as well turn round and give up.' He sits for another twenty seconds, then leans forward, opens the glove compartment and pulls out a stethoscope, which he hooks over the windscreen mirror. It hangs there like a skeleton, the membrane at the top, the metal and rubber leads dangling bow-legged, the two ivory ear-pieces clopping bonily against each other. He starts the engine, releases the handbrake, reverses two feet, then pulls out into the opposite side of the road.

'No,' says my mother again, half-heartedly. It could be that he is about to do a three-point turn and go back. No it couldn't...

My father does not drive particularly quickly past the marooned cars. No more than twenty miles an hour. Even so, it *feels* fast and arrogant, and all the occupants turn and stare as they see us coming. Some appear to be angry. Some are shouting. 'Point to the stethoscope, pet,' he tells my mother, but she has slid down sideways in her passenger seat, out of sight, her bottom resting on the floor, from where she berates him.

'God Almighty, Arthur, why do you have to do this? Why can't you wait like everyone else? What if we meet something coming the other way?' Now my sister and I do the same, hide ourselves below the seat. Our father is on his own. He is not with us, this bullying, shaming, undemocratic cheat, or rather, we are not with him.

My face pressed to the sweet-smelling upholstery, I imagine what is happening ahead. I can't tell how far we have gone, how many blind corners we have taken. If we meet something on this narrow country lane, we will have to reverse past all the cars we have just overtaken. I wait for the squeal of brakes.

After an eternity of – what? – two minutes, my mother sticks her head up and says, 'Now you've had it,' and my father replies, 'No, there's another gate beyond,' and my sister and I raise ourselves to look. We are level with the cars at the head of the queue, which are waiting to turn left into the brown ticket holder's entrance, the pleb's entrance. A steward steps out of the gateway towards us, but my father, pretending not to see him, drives past and on to a clear piece of road, where, two hundred yards ahead, the half a dozen cars that have come from the opposite direction are waiting to turn into another gateway. Unlike those we have left behind, these cars appear to be moving. Magnanimous, my father waits until the last one has turned in, then drives through the stone gateposts and over the bumpy grass to where an armbanded steward in a tweed jacket is waiting by the roped entrance.

'Good afternoon, sir. Red ticket holder?' The question does not come as a shock: we have all seen the signs, numerous and clamorous, saying RED TICKET HOLDERS' ENTRANCE. But my father is undeterred.

'These, you mean,' he says and hands over his brown tickets.

'No, sir, I'm afraid these are brown tickets.'

'But there must be some mistake. I applied for red tickets. To be honest, I didn't even look.'

'I'm sorry sir, but these are brown tickets, and brown's the next entrance, two hundred yards along. If you just swing round here, and...'

'I'm happy to pay the difference.'

'No, you see the rules say...'

'I know where the brown entrance is, I've just spent the last hour queueing for it by mistake. I drove up here because I thought I was red. I can't go back there now. The queue stretches for miles. And these children you know, who'd been looking forward...'

By now half a dozen cars have gathered behind us. One of them parps. The steward is wavering.

'You say you applied for red.'

'Not only applied for, paid for. I'm a doctor, you see...' – he points at the stethoscope – 'and I like being near the grandstand'.

This double *non-sequitur* seems to clinch it.

'All right, sir, but next time please check the tickets. Ahead and to your right.'

This is the way is was with my dad. Minor duplicities. Little fiddles. Money-saving, time-saving, privilege-attaining fragments of opportunism. The queue-jump, the backhander, the deal under the table. Parking where you shouldn't, drinking after hours, accepting the poached pheasant and the goods off the back of a lorry. 'They' were killjoys, after all – 'they' meaning the Establishment to which, despite being a middle-class professional, a GP, he never felt he belonged; our job as ordinary folk, trying to get the most out of life, was to outwit them. Serious law-breaking would have scared him, though he envied and often praised those who had pulled off ingenious, non-violent crimes, like the Great Train Robbers or, before them, the men who intercepted a lorry carrying a large number of old banknotes to the incinerator. ('Still in currency, you see, but not new, so there was no record of the numbers and they couldn't be traced. Brilliant, quite brilliant.') He was not himself up to being criminal in a big way but he'd have been lost if he couldn't cheat in a small way: so much of his pleasure derived from it. I grew up thinking it absolutely normal, that most Englishmen were like this. I still suspect that's the case.

BLAKE MORRISON

1 How would you describe the relationship between the writer's father and mother?

2 What does the writer feel towards his father – respect, awe, admiration, embarrassment, a sense of distance, affection? How can you tell?

COMPARE

Discussion

1 Working in small groups, discuss and note down the similarities and differences between the fathers in the two extracts.

2 What similarities can you find in the way males and females are treated differently in each text?

3 In your opinion which text is:

- more humorous
- more enjoyable
- more descriptive?

Working with a partner, find examples to support your ideas.

Assignments

1 What is *your* opinion of each of the two fathers in the extracts? Write a paragraph outlining your feelings and supporting them with examples.

2 Rewrite the extract from *Dombey and Son* from Florence Dombey's point of view. How would she react to the sight of her father with her new brother? Either update the language into modern English, or try to recreate Dickens's style.

3 Who most influenced you in your early childhood? Write your own account of memories of either your father or mother, giving examples which show what the relationship was like. Then add a paragraph explaining how your relationship has changed since then.

4 Interview one of your parents about your grandparents. Find out what your parent's sharpest memories are, how they were influenced, what they rebelled against. Then write up the interview either as a transcript (word-for-word account), or as a brief report.

THE CANTERBURY TALES

■ Five hundred years ago, Geoffrey Chaucer began a story which has been frequently retold, written about and studied ever since. The following three extracts come from different versions of the Prologue of *The Canterbury Tales*, in which the Knight, the first character to appear, is introduced.

The first extract comes from Chaucer's original version. Listen to it being read aloud, or read it aloud yourself.

1 In pairs, try and work out the modern English names of the places which the Knight has visited.

2 What do we learn about the character of the Knight?

A Knyght ther was

A KNYGHT ther was, and that a worthy man,
That fro the tyme that he first bigan
To riden out, he loved chivalrie,
Trouthe and honour, fredom and curteisie.
Ful worthy was he in his lordes werre,
And therto hadde he riden, no man ferre,
As wel in cristendom as in hethenesse,
And evere honoured for his worthynesse.
    At Alisaundre he was whan it was wonne.
Ful ofte tyme he hadde the bord bigonne
Aboven alle nacions in Pruce.
In Lettow hadde he reysed and in Ruce,
No Cristen man so ofte of his degree.
In Gernade at the seege eek hadde he be
Of Algezir, and riden in Belmarye.
At Lyeys was he and at Satalye,
Whan they were wonne; and in the Grete See
At many a noble armee hadde he be.
At mortal batailles hadde he been fiftene,
And foughten for oure feith at Tramyssene
In lystes thries, and ay slayn his foo.
This ilke worthy knyght hadde been also
Somtyme with the lord of Palatye
Agayn another hethen in Turkye,
And everemoore he hadde a sovereyn prys.
And though that he were worthy, he was wys,
And of his port as meeke as is a mayde.
He nevere yet no vileynye ne sayde
In al his lyf unto no maner wight.
He was a verray, parfit, gentil knyght.
But for to tellen yow of his array,
His hors weren goode, but he was nat gay.
Of fustian he wered a gypoun
Al bismotered with his habergeoun,
For he was late ycome from his viage,
And wente for to doon his pilgrymage.

GEOFFREY CHAUCER

■ This is a twentieth-century adaptation.

There was a Knight

THERE was a *Knight,* a most distinguished man,
Who from the day on which he first began
To ride abroad had followed chivalry,
Truth, honour, generousness and courtesy.
He had done nobly in his sovereign's war
And ridden into battle, no man more,
As well in Christian as in heathen places,
And ever honoured for his noble graces.
    When we took Alexandria, he was there.
He often sat at table in the chair
Of honour, above all nations, when in Prussia.
In Lithuania he had ridden, and Russia,
No Christian man so often, of his rank.
When, in Granada, Algeciras sank
Under assault, he had been there, and in
North Africa, raiding Benamarin;
In Anatolia he had been as well
And fought when Ayas and Attalia fell,
For all along the Mediterranean coast
He had embarked with many a noble host.
In fifteen mortal battles he had been
And jousted for our faith at Tramissene
Thrice in the lists, and always killed his man.
This same distinguished knight had led the van
Once with the Bey of Balat, doing work
For him against another heathen Turk;
He was of sovereign value in all eyes.
And though so much distinguished, he was wise
And in his bearing modest as a maid.
He never yet a boorish thing had said
In all his life to any, come what might;
He was a true, a perfect gentle-knight.
Speaking of his equipment, he possessed
Fine horses, but he was not gaily dressed.
He wore a fustian tunic stained and dark
With smudges where his armour had left mark;
Just home from service, he had joined our ranks
To do his pilgrimage and render thanks.

adapted by NEVILL COGHILL

AFTER READING

1 What details indicate that the story is set long ago?

2 List five points about the knight which you have learnt from this extract.

■ This version was written for children a hundred years ago.

A Knight there was

A KNIGHT there was, a very worthy man, from the time that he had first begun to ride about. He loved chivalry and truth, freedom and courtesy. He had borne with honour many high commands. He had been in Alexandria when it was won; had served with renown in Prussia, Russia, Turkey, and by the Great Sea; had fought in fifteen mortal battles, and in the lists of tourney for our faith had three times slain a foe. And though he was worthy he was also wise and modest. He never spoke evil, but was a very perfect, gentle knight. As for his array, his horse was good without being showy, and he wore a rough under-coat stained by his metal armour, for he had but lately arrived from a long voyage.

adapted by J WALKER McSPADDEN

AFTER READING

1 Pick out five words which still give the story an old-fashioned feeling.

2 Pick out five modern words which the writer has used.

COMPARE

Discussion

1 In pairs, look back at Chaucer's original language. Choose four lines and compare the way in which the two translators have adapted them. What do you notice about:

- the details which have been left in/out?
- the words which have been retained/changed?
- the rhythm of the lines?

2 The Knight is the first character mentioned by Chaucer at the beginning of *The Canterbury Tales*: how much does his presentation make you want to read on in each of the three versions?

3 From your reading of each of the versions, what impression do you get of:

- the narrator?
- the reader (or audience) being addressed?

Do the intended audiences seem to have different ages? How can you tell?

4 In pairs, prepare a choral reading which jumps from one version of the story to the next. As you change stories, use different speaking styles, e.g. a newsreader's voice, a poet's or a politician's, to create different effects.

Assignments

1 Devise a chart which shows the differences in the way the Knight is presented in each version. In which adaptation is his character most dissimilar to the original version?

2 Look back at the original extract. Choose a section; then, without referring to the adaptations, try to write your own version, in poetry or prose, updating it for a modern audience. When you have finished, write a paragraph explaining the problems you encountered.

3 Using notes made for previous answers, write a comparison of the three versions of Chaucer's story. You should focus on:

- the storyline
- the character of the Knight
- the amount of description
- unfamiliar words
- the difference between poetry and prose.

WIDER READING

Fiction
The following texts all contain strong central characters:

Charles Dickens, *Great Expectations*; Jane Austen, *Pride and Prejudice*; Sue Townsend, *The Secret Diary of Adrian Mole aged 13 ¾* ; Peter Benson, *The Levels*; Jane Gardam, *God on the Rocks*; Robert Westall, *The Scarecrows*.

Biography
Dirk Bogard, *Great Meadow*; Alice Thomas Ellis, *A Welsh Childhood*; Gerald Durrell, *My Family and Other Animals*; Polly Devlin, *The Far Side of the Lough*; Lesley Davies, *Lesley's Life*; Bob Geldof, *Is That It?*

1 Choose two characters from your reading and compare them – their looks, appearance, attitudes and lives.

2 Choose two biographies, and trace how two people develop during their lives – how do their attitudes and opinions change as they grow older?

SUGAR & SPICE, FROGS & SNAILS

In the nursery rhyme, girls are made of sugar and spice and all things nice; boys are made of frogs and snails and puppy dogs' tails.

- *Is this rhyme a harmless bit of fun, or is it evidence of something more serious?*
- *Do parents have different expectations for their daughters and their sons?*
- *How does society in general influence the choices that men and women are able to make about the way that they want to live their lives?*

BRINGING UP BOYS

■ Are differences in behaviour between girls and boys natural, or do children quickly learn what is expected of their sex?

The following poem and newspaper article suggest different ways of bringing up boys.

READING SKILLS
Reading for meaning
Summarising

If -

*If you can keep your head when all about you
Are losing theirs and blaming it on you,
If you can trust yourself when all men doubt you,
But make allowance for their doubting too;
If you can wait and not be tired by waiting,
Or being lied about, don't deal in lies,
Or being hated, don't give way to hating,
And yet don't look too good, nor talk too wise:*

*If you can dream – and not make dreams your master;
If you can think – and not make thoughts your aim;
If you can meet with Triumph and Disaster
And treat those two impostors just the same;
If you can bear to hear the truth you've spoken
Twisted by knaves to make a trap for fools,
Or watch the things you gave your life to, broken,
And stoop and build 'em up with worn-out tools:*

*If you can make one heap of all your winnings
And risk it on one turn of pitch-and-toss,
And lose, and start again at your beginnings*

AFTER READING

1 In pairs discuss what you think the poet means when he writes:

- *If you can keep your head when all about you Are losing theirs and blaming it on you*

and

- *If you can dream – and not make dreams your master; If you can think – and not make thoughts your aim*

2 Summarise what you think the poem's message is.

■ The following article examines the idea that girls and boys are born different.

And never breathe a word about your loss;
If you can force your heart and nerve and sinew
To serve your turn long after they are gone,
And so hold on when there is nothing in you
Except the Will which says to them: 'Hold on!'

If you can talk with crowds and keep your virtue,
Or walk with Kings – nor lose the common touch,
If neither foes nor loving friends can hurt you,
If all men count with you, but none too much;
If you can fill the unforgiving minute
With sixty seconds' worth of distance run,
Yours is the Earth and everything that's in it,
And – which is more – you'll be a Man, my son!

RUDYARD KIPLING

Boys will be Boys

<u>They turn household objects into weapons of war and believe they will grow up to be the boss. Do we blame their parents or is it in their make-up? Deborah Holder on the latest findings.</u>

WHAT happens if you show a group of adults a video of a nine-month-old child playing with a Jack-in-the-box, tell half of them the child is a boy and the other half it's a girl, then ask them to describe the child's behaviour? The result is a clear demonstration of the power of preconceptions. When the child reacts animatedly to the toy, those who believe it is a boy will describe the child's behaviour as anger; those who believe the child to be a girl will call it fear.

Few parents like the idea that they fall prey to sex-role

stereotyping, yet research suggests most do. Fathers are more vulnerable than mothers, particularly where sons are concerned. Although they are only slightly more concerned than mothers about their daughters doing traditionally "masculine" things, they are horrified by their sons doing "feminine" things. They are also more prone to emphasise the strength of their sons and the beauty and fragility of their daughters.

None of this is lost on the children themselves. Take child's play, for example. Countless experiments have found that, under the age of one, both sexes seem content to play with whatever is at hand. Later up to the age of five, girls show a much clearer interest in masculine toys than boys do in feminine ones. After this age, both sexes make increasingly sex-appropriate choices with the tendency even stronger in boys. Interestingly though, boys are more likely to experiment with girls' toys when they think nobody is looking.

Children clearly catch on fast, with a little help from parents and peers. They soon recognise that cultural taboos against effeminate behaviour in boys are stronger than those against masculine behaviour in girls. It's one

thing to be a tomboy, quite another to be a sissy. What is surprising is that children begin to absorb the preconceptions of those around them at such a tender age. In a recent American study, most two to three-year-olds agreed with the following generalisations: girls like to play with dolls, help their mothers, talk a lot, never hit, say "I need some help" and will grow up to be nurses or teachers; boys like to play with cars, help their dads, build things, say "I can hit you" and will grow up to be the boss.

An English report published a few months ago echoed these results. It found 46 per cent of six-year-old girls wanted to be nurses, and 30 per cent teachers. By the age of 10, 38 per cent of girls still wanted to be teachers while the other 60 per cent had moved on to hairdressing and air hostessing.

For some parents, apparent gender stereotyping is alarming and they feel the need to counteract it. But perhaps these children are simply following their instincts. If girls are naturally inclined towards caring professions and boys towards more active and "heroic" choices, then what right do parents or psychologists have to mess with this process? Aren't they doing so purely to satisfy their own ideologies?

Anne Moir, geneticist and co-author of *Brainsex: The Real Difference Between Men and Women*, argues that boys and girls make different choices, from toys to careers, because they simply are different and the difference begins in the womb. She dismisses "the vain contention that men and women are created the same" as "a Utopian fantasy", without which "men and women could live more happily and organise the world to better effect".

She cites decades of research by psychologists and physiologists, supporting the theory that the difference is biological and begins as early as six weeks after conception. The only reason this is not more widely accepted, she believes, is because it is a deeply unfashionable message in these politically correct times. She personally believes it is intellectually dishonest to deny it.

According to Moir, the brain is structured and "wired up" differently in males and females. They consequently process information differently and develop different perceptions, priorities and behaviours. It is the simple biological distinction, not social factors, that results in the gender differences we see from childhood.

One of the key ways in which the brains differ is that in women the left hemisphere, which deals with verbal skills, is dominant. In men the right hemisphere, specialising in visual, spatial and reasoning skills, predominates. This explains why men generally make better architects, map-readers and mathematicians, says Moir, while women tend to be better communicators.

The evidence of intellectual differences between the sexes has existed since testing began, but many psychologists claim these variations are now disappearing. The latest GCSE results seem to confirm this, with girls achieving only 1 per cent fewer passes than boys in science and 2 per cent fewer in maths. The figure for maths was 10 per cent in the early 1980s.

PARENTS often agonise over the question of nature versus nurture. Quite apart from the issue of sexism, there is something about the "biology is destiny" determinism of Anne Moir's argument that leaves a nasty taste. Before having children, parents-to-be often lean towards the view that boys and girls start out the same. It is only social pressures, they believe, that make children slip into traditional male and female roles. By adopting a consciously non-sexist approach, they reason – the right books and toys, non-gender-specific clothes – those who wish to can counter this.

A year or sometimes only a few months down the line, however, the same people can find themselves questioning their thinking on gender. Their beloved "blank slates", not as yet exposed to television or peer-group pressure, conform immediately to gender expectations. Boys seem more aggressive, capable of transforming the most innocuous household objects into weapons of war; girls come across as more verbal, sociable and affectionate creatures who do like dolls.

"Grace's toys were varied, her friends mixed and her books chosen to be non-sexist," says one mother, 33-year-old Jacqueline. "I didn't want to impose anything on her. On the contrary, I wanted to avoid the restrictions that conventional sex roles impose. But by the time she was a year old, she was seriously into dolls; as soon as she could walk, she wanted nothing more than to push the buggy at playgroup. She's less aggressive than the boys I see, and more affectionate. I see sensitive boys and aggressive girls, too – but not often."

THE INDEPENDENT ON SUNDAY

AFTER READING

1 Summarise the article in between three and five points.

2 Why do you think that fathers are only 'slightly more concerned than mothers about their daughters doing "masculine" things,' but are 'horrified by their sons doing "feminine" things'?

COMPARE

Discussion

1 In pairs, make a list of the qualities that Rudyard Kipling thinks a boy should develop in order to become a man. Then make a list of the criticisms that are made in the article about the ways that boys are brought up, and the effect that their upbringing has on their behaviour.

Compare the two lists. What differences and similarities can you find between the ideas of how boys should be brought up?

2 The newspaper article presents two sides of an argument: that boys and girls are naturally different, and that boys and girls are brought up to be different.

Make a list of points to back up each side of the argument.

Do some points in the first list contradict the points in the second? Discuss the contradictions in small groups and state which side of the argument you find to be the most convincing and why.

3 The article contains many words that have become common in the last twenty years to describe new ideas about men and women:

gender, masculine, feminine, non-sexist, sex-role, stereotyping.

If you are unsure about the meaning of any of these terms, discuss them with another pair, then look them up in a dictionary. Does the dictionary definition correspond to yours? Does it fit the way the words are used in the article? If the words are not in the dictionary, what does this tell you about them?

Assignments

1 'If' was written in the last century, and its language reflects this. Reread it carefully and pick out any clues which show that it was written in the Victorian age. What words would you use today to express the same ideas?

2 Write about a time when you were treated differently because of your sex. Choose a situation either at school or at home and describe in detail what happened.

3 Write a commentary on the language used in the poem and the language used in the newspaper article. You might want to consider the following points:

- What differences are there between the use of words in the poem, and in the article?
- How can you tell immediately that one is a poem and one is a newspaper article?
- Which use of language, in your view, is more effective and why?

4 Write a modern version of the poem, setting out the advice that you think parents should give to their children. Base your poem as closely as possible on the form of 'If'.

MISFITS

■ Neither of the women described in this section conform to their society's expectations of how girls and women should behave. In the first story, the old ladies of Toddsville relate the story of Esther Greenwood.

READING SKILLS

Developing personal response

Analysing language

The Unnatural Mother

'Don't tell me!' said old Mis' Briggs, with a forbidding shake of the head. 'No mother that was a mother would desert her own child for anything on earth!'

'And leaving it a care on the town, too!' put in Susannah Jacobs. 'As if we hadn't enough to do to take care of our own!'

Miss Jacobs was a well-to-do old maid, owning a comfortable farm and homestead, and living alone with an impoverished cousin acting as general servant, companion, and protégée. Mis' Briggs, on the contrary, had had thirteen children, five of whom remained to bless her, so that what maternal feeling Miss Jacobs might lack, Mis' Briggs could certainly supply.

'I should think,' piped little Martha Ann Simmons, the village dressmaker, 'that she might 'a saved her young one first and then tried what she could do for the town.'

Martha had been married, had lost her husband, and had one sickly boy to care for.

The youngest Briggs girl, still unmarried at thirty-six, and in her mother's eyes a most tender infant, now ventured to make a remark.

'You don't any of you seem to think what she did for all of us – if she hadn't left hers we should all have lost ours, sure.'

'You ain't no call to judge, Maria 'Melia,' her mother hastened to reply. 'You've no children of your own, and you can't judge of a mother's duty. No mother ought to leave her child, whatever happens. The Lord gave it to her to take care of – he never gave her other people's. You needn't tell me!'

'She was an unnatural mother,' repeated Miss Jacobs harshly, 'as I said to begin with!'

'What is the story?' asked the City Boarder. The City Boarder was interested in stories from a business point of view, but they did not know that. 'What did this woman do?' she asked.

There was no difficulty in eliciting particulars. The difficulty was rather in discriminating amidst their profusion and contradictoriness. But when the City Boarder got it clear in her mind, it was somewhat as follows:

The name of the much-condemned heroine was Esther Greenwood, and she lived and died here in Toddsville.

Toddsville was a mill village. The Todds lived on a beautiful eminence overlooking the little town, as the castles of robber barons on the Rhine used to overlook their little towns. The mills and the mill hands' houses were built close along the bed of the river. They had to be pretty close, because the valley was a narrow one, and the bordering hills were too steep for travel, but the water power was fine. Above the village was the reservoir, filling the entire valley save for a narrow road beside it, a fair blue smiling lake, edged with lilies and blue flag, rich in pickerel and perch. This lake gave them fish, it gave them ice, it gave the power that ran the mills that gave the town its bread. Blue Lake was both useful and ornamental.

In this pretty and industrious village Esther had grown up, the somewhat neglected child of a heart-broken widower. He had lost a young wife, and three fair babies before her – this one was left him, and he said he meant that she should have all the chance there was.

'That was what ailed her in the first place!' they all eagerly explained to the City Boarder. 'She never knew what 'twas to have a mother, and she grew up a regular tomboy! Why, she used to roam the country for miles around, in all weather like an Injun! And her father wouldn't take no advice!'

This topic lent itself to eager discussion. The recreant father, it appeared, was a doctor, not their accepted standby, the resident physician of the neighbourhood, but an alien doctor, possessed of 'views'.

'You never heard such things as he advocated,' Miss Jacobs explained. 'He wouldn't give no medicines, hardly; said "nature" did the curing – he couldn't.'

'And he couldn't either – that was clear,' Mrs Briggs agreed. 'Look at his wife and children dying on his hands, as it were! "Physician, heal thyself," I say.'

'But, Mother,' Maria Amelia put in, 'she was an invalid when he married her, they say; and those children died of polly – polly – what's that thing that nobody can help?'

'That may all be so,' Miss Jacobs admitted, 'but all the same, it's a doctor's business to give medicine. If "nature" was all that was wanted, we needn't have any doctor at all!'

'I believe in medicine and plenty of it. I always gave my children a good clearance, spring and fall, whether anything ailed 'em or not, just to be on the safe side. And if there was anything the matter with 'em, they had plenty more. I never had anything to reproach myself with on that score,' stated

Mrs Briggs, firmly. Then as a sort of concession to the family graveyard, she added piously, 'The Lord giveth and the Lord taketh away.'

'You should have seen the way he dressed that child!' pursued Miss Jacobs. 'It was a reproach to the town. Why, you couldn't tell at a distance whether it was a boy or a girl. And barefoot! He let that child go barefoot till she was so big we was actually mortified to see her.'

It appeared that a wild, healthy childhood had made Esther very different in her early womanhood from the meek, well-behaved damsels of the little place. She was well enough liked by those who knew her at all, and the children of the place adored her, but the worthy matrons shook their heads and prophesied no good of a girl who was 'queer'.

She was described with rich detail in reminiscence, how she wore her hair short till she was fifteen – 'just shingled like a boy's – it did seem a shame that girl had no mother to look after her – and her clo'se was almost a scandal, even when she did put on shoes and stockings. Just gingham – brown gingham and *short!*'

'I think she was a real nice girl,' said Maria Amelia. 'I can remember her just as well! She was so nice to us children. She was five or six years older that I was, and most girls that age won't have anything to do with little ones. But she was kind and pleasant. She'd take us berrying and on all sorts of walks, and teach us new games and tell us things. I don't remember anyone that ever did us the good she did!'

Maria Amelia's thin chest heaved with emotion, and there were tears in her eyes; but her mother took her up somewhat sharply.

'That sounds well I must say – right before your own mother that's toiled and slaved for you! It's all very well for a young thing that's got nothing on earth to do to make herself agreeable to young ones. That poor blinded father of hers never taught her to do the work a girl should – naturally he couldn't.'

'At least he might have married again and given her another mother,' said Susannah Jacobs, with decision, with so much decision, in fact, that the City Boarder studied her expression for a moment and concluded that if this recreant father had not married again it was not for lack of opportunity.

Mrs Simmons cast an understanding glance upon Miss Jacobs, and nodded wisely.

'Yes, he ought to have done that, of course. A man's not fit to bring up children, anyhow. How can they? Mothers have the instinct – that is, all natural mothers have. But, dear me! There's some as don't seem to be mothers – even when they have a child!'

'You're quite right, Mis' Simmons,' agreed the mother of thirteen. 'It's a divine instinct, I say. I'm sorry for the child that lacks it. Now this Esther. We always knew she wan't like other girls – she never seemed to care for dress and company and things girls naturally do, but was always philandering over the hills with a parcel of young ones. There wan't a child in town but would run after her. She made more trouble 'n a little in families, the young ones quotin' what Aunt Esther said, and tellin' what Aunt Esther did to their own mothers, and she only a young girl. Why, she actually seemed to care more for them children than she did for beaux or anything – it wasn't natural!'

'But she did marry?' pursued the City Boarder.

'Marry! Yes, she married finally. We all thought she never would, but she did. After the things her father taught her, it did seem as if he'd ruined *all* her chances. It's simply terrible the way that girl was trained.'

'Him being a doctor,' put in Mrs Simmons, 'made it different, I suppose.'

'Doctor or no doctor,' Miss Jacobs rigidly interposed, 'it was a crying shame to have a young girl so instructed.'

'Maria 'Melia,' said her mother, 'I want you should get me my smelling salts. They're up in the spare chamber, I believe. When your Aunt Marcia was here she had one of her spells – don't you remember? – and she asked for salts. Look in the top bureau drawer – they must be there.'

Maria Amelia, thirty-six but unmarried, withdrew dutifully, and the other ladies drew closer to the City Boarder.

'It's the most shocking thing I ever heard of,' murmured Mrs Briggs. 'Do you know he – a father – actually taught his daughter how babies come!'

There was a breathless hush.

'He did,' eagerly chimed in the little dressmaker. 'All the particulars. It was perfectly awful!'

'He said,' continued Mrs Briggs, 'that he expected her to be a mother and that she ought to understand what was before her!'

'He was waited on by a committee of ladies from the church, married ladies, all older than he was,' explained Miss Jacobs severely. 'They told him it was creating a scandal in the town and what do you think he said?'

There was another breathless silence.

Above, the steps of Maria Amelia were heard, approaching the stairs.

'It ain't there, Ma!'

'Well, you look in the highboy and in the top drawer; they're somewhere up there,' her mother replied.

Then, in a sepulchral whisper:

'He told us – yes, ma'am, I was on that committee – he told us that until young women knew what was before them as mothers, they would not do their duty in choosing a father for their children! That was his expression – "choosing a father"! A nice thing for a young girl to be thinking of – a father for her children!'

'Yes, and more than that,' inserted Miss Jacobs, who, though not on the committee, seemed familiar with its workings. 'He told them –' But Mrs Briggs waved her aside and continued swiftly –

'He taught that innocent girl about – the Bad Disease! Actually!'

'He did!' said the dressmaker. 'It got out, too, all over town. There wasn't a man here would have married her after that.'

Miss Jacobs insisted on taking up the tale. 'I understand that he said it was "to protect her"! Protect her, indeed! Against matrimony! As if any man alive would want to marry a young girl who knew all the evil of life! I was brought up differently, I assure you!'

'Young girls should be kept innocent!' Mrs Briggs solemnly proclaimed. 'Why, when I was married I knew no more what was before me than a babe unborn, and my girls were all brought up so, too!'

Then, as Maria Amelia returned with the salts, she continued more loudly. 'But she did marry after all. And a mighty queer husband she got, too. He was an artist or something, made pictures for the magazines and such as that, and they do say she met him first out in the hills. That's the first 'twas known of it here, anyhow – them two traipsing about all over; him with his painting things! They married and just settled down to live with her father, for she vowed she wouldn't leave him; and he said it didn't make no difference where he lived, he took his business with him.'

'They seemed very happy together,' said Maria Amelia. 'Happy! Well, they might have been, I suppose. It was a pretty queer family, I think.' And her mother shook her head in retrospection. 'They got on all right for a while; but the old man died, and those two – well, I don't call it housekeeping the way they lived!'

'No,' said Miss Jacobs. 'They spent more time out-of-doors than they did in the house. She followed him around everywhere. And for open lovemaking –'

They all showed deep disapproval at this memory. All but the City Boarder and Maria Amelia.

'She had one child, a girl,' continued Mrs Briggs, 'and it was just shocking to see how she neglected that child from the beginnin'. She never seemed to have no maternal feelin' at all!'

'But I though you said she was very fond of children,' remonstrated the City Boarder.

'Oh, *children*, yes. She'd take up with any dirty-faced brat in town, even them Canucks. I've seen her again and again with a whole swarm of the mill hands' young ones round her, goin' on some picnic or other – "open air school", she used to call it – *such* notions as she had. But when it come to her own child! Why -' Here the speaker's voice sank to a horrified husk. 'She never had no baby clo'se for it! Not a single sock!'

The City Boarder was interested. 'Why, what did she do with the little thing?

'The Lord knows!' answered old Mis' Briggs. 'She never would let us hardly see it when 'twas little. 'Shamed too, I don't doubt. But that's strange feelin's for a mother. Why, I was so proud of my babies! And I kept 'em lookin' so pretty! I'd 'a sat up all night and sewed and washed, but I'd 'a had my children look well!' And the poor old eyes filled with tears as she thought of the eight little graves in the churchyard, which she never failed to keep looking pretty, even now. 'She just let that young one roll round in the grass like a puppy with hardly nothin' on! Why, a squaw does better. She does keep 'em done up for a spell! The child was treated worse 'n an Injun! We all done what we could, of course. We felt it no more 'n right. But she was real hateful about it, and we had to let her be.'

'The child died?' asked the City Boarder.

'Died! Dear no! That's it you saw going by; a great strappin' girl she is, too, and promisin' to grow up well, thanks to Mrs Stone's taking her. Mrs Stone always thought a heap of Esther. It's a mercy to the child that she lost her mother, I do believe! How she ever survived that kind of treatment beats all! Why, that woman never seemed to have their first spark of maternal feeling to the end! She seemed just as fond of the other young ones after she had her own as she was before, and that's against nature. The way it happened was this. You see, they lived up the valley nearer to the lake than the village. He was away, and was coming home that night, it seems, driving from Drayton along the lake road. And she set out to meet him. She must 'a walked up to the dam to look for him; and we think maybe she saw the team clear across the lake. Maybe she thought he could get to the house and save little Esther in time – that's the only explanation we ever could put on it. But this is what she did; and you can judge for yourselves if any mother in her senses *could* 'a done such a thing! You see 'twas the time of that awful disaster, you've read of it, likely, that destroyed three villages. Well, she got to the dam and seen that 'twas givin' way – she was always great for knowin' all such things. And she just turned and ran. Jake Elder was up on the hill after a stray cow, and he seen her go. He was too far off to imagine what ailed her, but he said he never saw a woman run so in his life.

'And, if you'll believe it, she run right by her own house – never stopped – never looked at it. Just run for the village. Of course, she may have lost her head with the fright, but that wasn't like her. No, I think she had made up her mind to leave that innocent baby to die! She just ran down here and give warnin', and, of course, we sent word down valley on horseback, and there was no lives lost in all three villages. She started to run back as soon as we was 'roused, but 'twas too late then.

'Jake saw it all, though he was too far off to do a thing. He said he couldn't stir a foot, it was so awful. He seen the wagon drivin' along as nice as you please till it got close to the dam, and then Greenwood seemed to see the danger and shipped up like mad. He was the father, you know. But he wasn't quite in time – the dam give way and the water went over him like a tidal wave. She was almost to the gate when it struck the house and her – and we never found her body nor his for days and days. They was washed clear down river.

'Their house was strong, and it stood a little high and had some big trees between it and the lake, too. It was moved off the place and brought up against the side of the stone church down yonder, but 'twant wholly in pieces. And that child was found swimmin' round in its bed, most drowned, but not quite. The wonder is, it didn't die of a cold, but it's

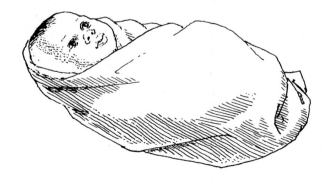

here yet – must have a strong constitution. Their folks never did nothing for it – so we had to keep it here.'

'Well, now, Mother,' said Maria Amelia Briggs. 'It does seem to me that she did her duty. You know yourself that if she hadn't give warnin' all three of the villages would 'a been cleaned out – a matter of fifteen hundred people. And if she'd stopped to lug that child, she couldn't have got here in time. Don't you believe she was thinkin' of those mill hands' children?'

'Maria 'Melia, I'm ashamed of you!' said old Mis' Briggs. 'But you ain't married and ain't a mother. A mother's duty is to her own child! She neglected her own to look after other folks' – the Lord never gave her them other children to care for!'

'Yes,' said Miss Jacobs, 'and here's her child, a burden on the town! She was an unnatural mother!'

CHARLOTTE PERKINS GILMAN

The Mill On The Floss

'But,' continued Mr Tulliver, after a pause, 'what I'm a bit afraid on is, as Tom hasn't got the right sort o' brains for a smart fellow. I doubt he's a bit slowish. He takes after your family, Bessy.'

'Yes, that he does,' said Mrs Tulliver, accepting the last proposition entirely on its own merits; 'he's wonderful for liking a deal o' salt in his broth. That was my brother's way, and my father's before him.'

'It seems a bit of a pity, though, said Mr Tulliver, 'as the lad should take after the mother's side istead o' the little wench. That's the worst on't wi' the crossing o'breeds: you can never justly calkilate what'll come on't. The little un takes after my side, now: she's twice as 'cute as Tom. Too 'cute for a woman, I'm afraid,' continued Mr Tulliver, turning his head dubiously first on one side and then on the other. 'It's no mischief much while she's a little un, but an over-'cute woman's no better nor a long-tailed sheep – she'll fetch none the bigger price for that.'

'Yes it *is* a mischief while she's a little un, Mr Tulliver, for it all runs to naughtiness. How to keep her in a clean pinafore two hours together passes my cunning. An' now you put me i' mind,' continued Mrs Tulliver, rising and going to the window, 'I don't know

AFTER READING

1 How many people are discussing Esther Greenwood? Who are they?

2 Discuss, in pairs, the choice that Esther made when she saw that the dam was about to burst. Do you think that she did the right thing?

■ Mr and Mrs Tulliver have two children, Tom, the older boy, and Maggie, his younger sister. At this point in the story Mr Tulliver has decided to send Tom to boarding school. Although Maggie is obviously more able than Tom, she will not receive an education.

where she is now, an' it's pretty nigh teatime. Ah, I thought so – wanderin' up an' down by the water, like a wild thing: she'll tumble in some day.'

Mrs Tulliver rapped the window sharply, beckoned, and shook her head, – a process which she repeated more than once before she returned to her chair.

'You talk o' 'cuteness, Mr Tulliver,' she observed as she sat down, 'but I'm sure the child's half an idiot i' some things; for if I send her up-stairs to fetch anything, she forgets what she's gone for, an' perhaps 'ull sit down on the floor i' the sunshine an' plait her hair an' sing to herself like a Bedlam creatur', all the while I'm waiting for her down-stairs. That niver run i' my family, thank God, no more nor a brown skin as makes her look like a mulatter. I don't like to fly i' the face o' Providence, but it seems hard as I should have but one gell, an' her so comical.'

'Pooh, nonsense!' said Mr Tulliver, 'she's a straight black-eyed wench as anybody need wish to see. I don't know i' what she's behind other folks's children; and she can read almost as well as the parson.'

'But her hair won't curl all I can do with it, and she's so franzy about having it put i' paper, and I've such work as never was to make her stand and have it pinched with th' irons.'

'Cut it off – cut it off short,' said the father, rashly. 'How can you talk, so Mr Tulliver? She's too big a gell, gone nine, and tall of her age, to have her hair cut short; an' there's her cousin Lucy's got a row o' curls round her head, an' not a hair out o' place. It seems hard as my sister Deane should have that pretty child; I'm sure Lucy takes more after me nor my own child does. Maggie, Maggie,' continued the mother, in a tone of half-coaxing fretfulness, as this small mistake of nature entered the room, 'where's the use o' my telling you to keep away from the water? You'll tumble in and be drowned some day, an' then you'll be sorry you didn't do as mother told you.'

Maggie's hair, as she threw off her bonnet, painfully confirmed her mother's accusation: Mrs Tulliver, desiring her daughter to have a curled crop, 'like other folks's children,' had it cut too short in front to be pushed behind the ears; and it was usually straight an hour after it had been taken out of paper, Maggie was incessantly tossing her head to keep the dark heavy locks out of her gleaming black eyes – an action which gave her very much the air of a small Shetland pony.

'O dear, O dear, Maggie, what are you thinkin' of, to throw your bonnet down there? Take it up-stairs, there's a good gell, an' let your hair be brushed, an' put your other pinafore on, an' change your shoes – do, for shame; an' come an' go on with your patch-work, like a little lady.'

'O mother,' said Maggie, in a vehemently cross tone, 'I don't *want* to do my patchwork.'

'What! not your pretty patchwork, to make a counterpane for your aunt Glegg?'

'It's foolish work,' said Maggie, with a toss of her mane, – 'tearing things to pieces to sew 'em together again. And I don't want to do anything for my aunt Glegg – I don't like her.'

Exit Maggie, dragging her bonnet by the string, while Mr Tulliver laughs audibly.

'I wonder at you, as you'll laugh at her, Mr Tulliver,' said the mother, with feeble fretfulness in her tone. 'You encourage her i' naughtiness. An' her aunts will have it as it's me spoils her.'

GEORGE ELIOT

AFTER READING

1 What are Maggie's faults according to her mother?

2 What does Mr Tulliver mean when he says 'an over-'cute woman's no better nor a long-tailed sheep – she'll fetch none the bigger price for that'?

COMPARE

Discussion

1 What do Esther Greenwood and Maggie Tulliver have in common? Discuss this in pairs, and find evidence from the two texts to support your views.

2 Who, in your opinion, has done the better job of bringing up their child? Dr Greenwood or Mrs Tulliver? Give reasons for your view.

3 Imagine that Mrs Briggs and Mrs Tulliver have met and have begun a conversation about Esther's and Maggie's faults, and the proper way to bring girls up. In pairs, discuss what they might talk about, and then prepare a role play on this topic. Look carefully at the way that they both speak, and try to imitate them. When you have performed your role play, write your own version of their conversation.

Assignments

1 Choose to work on either *The Unnatural Mother* or *The Mill On The Floss*. Choose a section of conversation which is about fifteen lines long, then rewrite this conversation in standard English. Compare your modern version with the original conversation. What differences, if any, has this made to the way you judge the characters? Are their opinions more convincing when expressed in standard English? If so, why? Are there any other differences that you notice between the effect of the two versions?

2 What is it about being a girl or being a boy which most annoys you? Write an essay answering this question, explaining also what you think could be done to improve the situation.

DILEMMAS OF LOVE

■ Girls and boys often have very little to do with each other until they fall in love, but the promise of early passion is not always fulfilled. These poems, one from a man's point of view and one from a woman's, explore two different sides to love. In the first an Angolan poet addresses his beloved.

LETTER FROM A CONTRACT WORKER

I wanted to write you a letter
my love
a letter to tell
of this longing
to see you
and this fear
of losing you
of this thing which deeper than I want, I feel
a nameless pain which pursues me
a sorrow wrapped about my life.

I wanted to write you a letter
my love
a letter of intimate secrets
a letter of memories of you
of you
your lips as red as the tacula fruit
your hair black as the dark diloa fish
your eyes gentle as the macongue
your breasts hard as young maboque fruit
your light walk
your caresses
better than any that I find down here.

I wanted to write you a letter
my love
to bring back our days together in our secret haunts
nights lost in the long grass
to bring back the shadow of your legs
and the moonlight filtering through the endless palms,
to bring back the madness of our passion
and the bitterness of separation.

I wanted to write you a letter
my love
which you could not read without crying
which you would hide from your father Bombo
and conceal from your mother Kieza
which you would read without the indifference

of forgetfulness,
a letter which would make any other
in all Kilombo worthless.

I wanted to write you a letter
my love
a letter which the passing wind would take
a letter which the cashew and the coffee trees,
the hyenas and the buffalo,
the caymans and the river fish
could hear
the plants and the animals
pitying our sharp sorrow
from song to song
lament to lament
breath to caught breath
would leave to you, pure and hot,
the burning
the sorrowful words of the letter
I wanted to write you.

I wanted to write you a letter.
But my love, I don't know why it is,
why, why, why it is, my love,
but you can't read
and I – oh the hopelessness – I can't write.

ANTONIO JACUNTI
Translated from the Portuguese by Margaret Dickinson

AFTER READING

1 Look again at each verse of the poem. Write a list of the main reasons (one for each verse) why the poet wants to write his love a letter.

2 What words or phrases are repeated in the poem? What effect is created by their repetition?

MANWATCHING

From across the party I watch you,
Watching her.
Do my possessive eyes
Imagine your silent messages?
I think not.
She looks across at you
And telegraphs her flirtatious reply.
I have come to recognize this code,
You are on intimate terms with this pretty stranger,
And there is nothing I can do,
My face is calm, expressionless,

But my eyes burn into your back.
While my insides shout with rage.
She weaves her way towards you,
Turning on a bewitching smile.
I can't see your face, but you are mesmerised I expect.
I can predict you: I know this scene so well,
Some acquaintance grabs your arm,
You turn and meet my accusing stare head on,
Her eyes follow yours, meet mine,
And then slide away, she understands,
She's not interested enough to compete.
It's over now.
She fades away, you drift towards me,
'I'm bored' you say, without a trace of guilt,
So we go.
Passing the girl in the hall.
'Bye' I say frostily,
I suppose
You winked.

GEORGIA GARRETT

1 Why is this poem called 'Manwatching'?

2 What, in one phrase or sentence, is it about?

COMPARE

Discussion

1 In pairs, work out the story behind each poem.

2 What emotions are being expressed in each of the poems? For each emotion that you identify, pick a line from the poem that you feel expresses this emotion most effectively. Which poem is more emotional? Which seems more sincere?

3 Look again at each of the poems, and work out what you think is meant by each of the following lines:

*   *...I feel*
    a nameless pain which pursues me
    a sorrow wrapped about my life.
*   *which you would read without the indifference*
    of forgetfulness
*   *Do my possessive eyes*
    Imagine your silent messages?
*   *She looks across at you*
    And telegraphs her flirtatious reply.
    I have come to recognize this code.

Assignments

1 Both poets use particular language devices, such as repetition, alliteration, personification and simile, in order to convey particularly important points. Look through the poems to find examples of these devices. Why has each poet used them?

2 Write the next part of the story of the poem 'Manwatching'.

3 Write a comparison of the narrators of each poem – their characters, outlooks and attitudes towards the people they are addressing, as well as their attitudes towards love.

THE TAMING OF THE SHREW

■ Katherina is the 'shrew' of the title. She is a strong woman who is used to expressing her views and to doing what she wants to do. She is forced by her father to marry Petruchio and he has been bribed to marry Katherina. In his efforts to 'tame' his wife and make her show what he thinks is proper respect for her husband, Petruchio has starved her, deprived her of sleep and kept her dressed in rags. This is the final speech of the play. In it, Katherina tells the audience how she now thinks that women should behave towards men.

To make it easier to analyse, the speech has been separated into four sections.

Practise reading it aloud.

READING SKILLS
Reading aloud
Reading for meaning

KATHERINA'S SPEECH

A   Thy husband is thy lord, thy life, thy keeper,
Thy head, thy sovereign; one that cares for thee,
And for thy maintenance commits his body
To painful labour both by sea and land,
To watch the night in storms, the day in cold,
Whilst thou liest warm at home, secure and safe;
And craves no other tribute at thy hands
But love, fair looks, and true obedience
Too little payment for so great a debt.

B   Such duty as the subject owes the prince,
Even such a woman oweth to her husband;
And when she is froward, peevish, sullen, sour,
And not obedient to his honest will,
What is she but a foul contending rebel
And graceless traitor to her loving lord?

C   I am asham'd that women are so simple
To offer war when they should kneel for peace;
Or seek for rule, supremacy, and sway,
When they are bound to serve, love, and obey.
Why are our bodies soft and weak and smooth,
Unapt to toil and trouble in the world,
But that our soft conditions and our hearts
Should well agree with our external parts?

D   Come, come, you froward and unable worms!
       My mind has been as big as one of yours,
       My heart as great, my reason haply more,
       To bandy word for word and frown for frown;
       But now I see our lances are but straws,
       Our strength as weak, our weakness past compare,
       That seeming to be most which we indeed least are.
       Then vail your stomachs, for it is no boot,
       And place your hands below your husband's foot;
       In token of which duty, if he please,
       My hand is ready, may it do him ease.

WILLIAM SHAKESPEARE

AFTER READING

1 What mood is Katherina in when she makes this speech. Is she resigned, bitter, content, sincere? How can you tell?

Discussion

1   Working in groups of four discuss your interpretation and prepare a reading of Katherina's speech to read aloud to the rest of the class. Each member of the group should choose one of the four sections. Copy out your section, then work in pairs to decide how you are going to say the lines. Mark up your section so that you can remember the decisions that you made. The following signs might be helpful:

Underline the words or phrases that you want to emphasise.
Mark with a // all the points where you want to pause.
Mark with a — the points where you think that the lines should 'run on'.

Practise the reading of the speech in your group, and then perform it in front of the rest of the class.

2   Look again at *your* section of the speech. Write a commentary on your markings saying why you chose to emphasise certain words and phrases, to pause at particular points and to run certain lines together.

Assignments

1   Look again at section A of the speech. Make a list of the words that Katherina uses when she describes a husband. What does this tell you of the relationship that she thinks should exist between husbands and wives?

Look at section B
Make a list of the words that Katherina uses in this section to describe those women who do not treat their husbands as 'Lords'. What picture is Katherina attempting to paint of these women through her choice of words in this section?

Look at section C
What reasons does Katherina put forward to back up her argument that women should be subservient to men?

Look at section D
What lines in this section tell us that Katherina did not always believe that men were superior to women?

2   Katherina directs much of this speech to her younger sister Bianca who does not always obey her husband unquestioningly. Imagine that you are Bianca. Write the speech that she would make in response to Katherina. You can write in either prose or verse. When you have finished, read out your speech to your group, or to the rest of the class.

WIDER READING

Fiction

The following stories are about girls and boys who do not agree with what their parents have planned for their lives:

Robert Leeson, *It's My Life*; Timothy Ireland, *Who Lies Inside?*; Louise Fitzhurg, *Nobody's Family Is Going To Change*; Maxine Hong Kingston, *The Woman Warrior*.

In these stories women rebel against what society expects of them:

Anthony Trollope, *Can You Forgive Her?*; D.H.Lawrence, *Women in Love*; Ruth Prawer Jhabvala, *Heat and Dust*; Charlotte Brontë, *Jane Eyre*; Charlotte Perkins Gillman, *Turned*.

Poetry

Yesterday, Today, Tomorrow (an anthology).

AFTER READING

1 Do you think that the stories you have read are realistic or are they far-fetched? Give reasons for your view.

2 Write your own story in which a girl or a boy refuses to conform to what society expects of them.

TRAVEL

Nowadays we tend to take travelling for granted – we use cars, bikes, trains and buses almost without noticing. But for many people there is still a thrill in 'real' travel, in exploring new places and cultures.
- *Why do some people still feel the need to make long and dangerous journeys?*
- *Do travellers wish to discover unfamiliar places or escape from too-familiar ones?*

TO INDIA

■ These two extracts show contrasting images of travel in India – the first from a holiday brochure, the second from a traveller.

READING SKILLS
Analysing language
Distinguishing fact from fiction/detecting bias
Studying genre

TAJ MAHAL
& The Pink City

Outstanding among the Wonders of the World – the much appreciated Taj Mahal, crafted out of white marble, is of course a tribute to the undying love of Shahjehan. It has become a universal symbol of love. This comprehensive excursion, with air transfer, takes in the finest sites on the northern circuit, history ancient and modern – dating back over 2000 years and finishing in Delhi.

DAY 1:   SUN
DEPARTURE FLIGHT

London – Gatwick (North Terminal) on the Caledonian Airways overnight flight for Goa. This tour begins and ends in Goa, combining the challenge of 7 nights of cultural input, with 7 more to relax and reflect upon, down on the beach.

DAY 2:   MON
AURANGABAD

On arrival, met and transferred to City Hotel for freshen-up. Afternoon transfer to the Airport, fly to Aurangabad. On arrival met and transfer to the Hotel Ambassador for overnight.

DAY 3:   TUE
AJANTA CAVES

Morning departure for a full days excursion, first 112kms to Ajanta Caves. The caves here consist of 24 monasteries (Viharas) and 5 temples, thought to be over 2,000 years old and hewn out of solid rock. The outstanding wall paintings and frescoes of these caves provide a wealth of colour and a beautiful flow of lines, worked with an overwhelming sense of vitality. They were discovered by a British hunting party in the 19th century and provide insight into the thinking of the followers of a Buddhist order – thought to date from about 200BC – 650AD. Return to Aurangabad with overnight at the Ambassador Hotel.

DAY 4:   WED
ELLORA CAVES

Today we journey to Ellora Caves – temples relating the development of Hinduism, Janism and Buddhism; chiselled by Monks out of solid rock. The most outstanding is the stupendous rocky temple of Kailash, comparing favourably with the pyramids of Egypt. Freshen-up back at the hotel. Later met and transferred to the Airport for your flight to Agra. On arrival met and transferred to the Ashok Hotel for overnight stay.

DAY 5:   THUR
AGRA

In the morning we visit 'one of the seven wonders of the world' – The Taj Mahal, built by Emperor Shahjehan as a mausoleum for his Queen Mumtaz Mahal in white marble – it has become 'a universal symbol of love'. Agra Fort is a testimony to the rise and fall of the Imperial Moghul Empire. It contains the Palaces of Dewan-e-Khas *House of Lords*, Dewen-e-Aaam *House of Commons* and Pearl Mosque, Moti Masjid. Also the Jasmine Tower & Itmad-ud-Daulah. Afternoon at leisure for shopping and overnight at the Ashok Hotel.

DAY 6:   FRI
JAIPUR – The Pink City

There is a popular saying in Jaipur: *'to be a man one must know how to wield the sword, the pen and the brush'.* Our morning drive there takes us via the deserted City of Fatehpur Sikri, perfectly preserved – built to commemorate the birth of Akbar's son – a symbol of fusion of the Indo-Saracenic architecture and radiating an atmosphere of incomparable beauty and majesty. On to Jaipur – on arrival check in at the Jaipur Palace Hotel. Also known as the Pink City, our afternoon tour of Jaipur takes in the City Palace Museum. On to the 'Palace of Winds', Jantar Mantar Observatory, built in 1726. Overnight is at the Jaipur Palace Hotel.

DAY 7:   SAT
DELHI

Morning drive to Amber Fort, ancient capital of the Rajput Empire en route to Delhi. Time for an exhilarating ride atop an Indian elephant! – optional if available! On arrival in Delhi check in at the Kanishka Hotel for overnight stay.

AFTER READING

1 Pick out three sentences or phrases which indicate that this is a holiday brochure.

2 Discuss what you think is the ratio of fact to opinion (e.g. 50:50).

■ Liz Maudslay made her first trip to India as a student in 1968. Since then she has repeatedly returned, often for several months, and has worked and travelled in many different regions. In this extract she describes travelling across Kashmir, a geographical region between India and Pakistan.

DAY 8:	SUN

DELHI

Our tour of majestic Delhi – a City of architectural contrasts – begins in Old Delhi where we visit the Jama Masjid. Our drive then takes us through fabled Chandni Chowk visiting Red Fort, Raj Ghat, Gandhi Memorial Museum and Feroz Shah Kotia, ruins of the fortress where we can see an Askoka Pillar. Our visit of New Delhi incorporates visiting Quatab Minar, Humayun's Tomb, Government buildings, and our drive takes us past the Raj Path, India Gate, President's Residence, Parliament House, Birla Mandir through Connaught Place. P.M. to shop, overnight, Kanishka Hotel.

DAY 9:	MON

GOA

In the morning, met and transferred to the airport for your flight to Goa; met and transferred to the beach hotel or your choice for the next seven nights.

SOMAK HOLIDAYS

Trekking from Kashmir

"You want houseboat? Five star deluxe. Bathroom attached. Very good houseboat. Very cheap." Arrival in Srinigar can seem the antithesis of the imagined Shangri-la where delicately carved boats rest on tranquil lakes surrounded by snow-peaked mountains. The boats and lakes and mountains are all there. So is the hassling. Tourism has created it; generations of tourists, Indian and Western. And then, unjust but inevitable, it is the tourists who most resent it. However, far from all Kashmiris are the unscrupulous grabbers they are made out to be by the generalising, besieged traveller.

On recent visits I have stayed on a houseboat owned by one of the kindest and most honest families I have ever met. The son, Rashid, also shares my passion for walking and climbing. He regularly takes tourists for short treks and it was while we were talking about these that we developed the plan of sharing a much longer and less frequented trek. We both needed each other for this. I would finance the expedition, paying for the pony men whom he could not otherwise afford, while he would be able to act as guide and translator.

A rich variety of treks can begin in Kashmir, including

those which go on into the barer regions of Ladakh and Zanskar. This time we decided to stay in Kashmir and walk from Sonamarg in the north to Bandipur in the west, near the Pakistan border. We estimated this would take us about three weeks.

Unlike Nepal, Kashmir does not have the same small villages where you can find board and lodging; hence you need to take a tent and all your food, and on a longer trek this means pack ponies. Rashid's father, Habib, has been walking in the mountains since he was a boy and knew exactly how much of everything we would need. The whole family joined us in packing up gunny bags full of rice, lentils, tea, oats, sugar and salt and measuring out bottles of kerosene. The next day we caught a bus to Sonamarg where we negotiated with two pony men.

It rained solidly for three days in Sonamarg. Three days of waiting in the tent with only occasional drenched sorties splashing through the mud river of the one main street to by bread or milk. This can be a problem with Kashmiri treks. The months when the high passes are open are July to September but these are by no means the driest. However, on the fourth day a watery sun emerged and we set off along slippery paths. As we climbed up through the steaming green forest I began to get to know the pony men.

"Why was I wanting to walk in the mountains at all, especially on a route which no one was quite sure of and which no one they knew had ever walked before?"

Manikar was elderly with a grizzled face, very bright eyes, and a thin body which I soon realised would be able to outwalk any of us. He had been on numerous treks and this, along with his age, gave him a licence to tease and play. Aziz was younger and shyer. He had black curly hair and incredibly gentle large brown eyes which would flow through expressions ranging from enjoyment, to bewilderment, embarrassment and shock at Manikar's excesses. Those were my impressions of them but what were theirs of me? Manikar's previous treks had all been with groups of foreigners. Why was I a woman alone? Where was my husband or brother? Why was I wanting to walk in the mountains at all, especially on a route which no one was quite sure of and which no one they knew had ever walked before? Their way of coping with the situation was for Manikar to become my "father", Aziz my "brother" while

Rashid could be the "guide". I accepted my role as daughter and sister. I knew it was the only way which would allow us to become close.

We walked through the forest which smelled of damp pine and up above the treeline to where the grass changed into the dirty snow edge of a glacier. Kashmiri shepherd villages comprise just one or two husks made up of pine trunks and built into the mountainside so that they are six or seven feet high at the front and three or four feet at the back. There are no windows, only a space for a door, and the dank inside smells of the sweet pine needles which make up the floor. The roof is pressed earth where the goats are herded at night. They are inhabited in the summer months by Gujar shepherds who come up from the plains.

This village had only one hut, inhabited by a shepherd, his wife and daughter. As we pitched our tents he came up to talk and asked if I had any medicines for his daughter. This was the first of many such requests and I always felt uneasy and inadequate with the role of the Western omnipotent doctor. But it was also one way in which I could talk easily to the women who otherwise tended to hide shyly as their husbands approached. The daughter was about twelve years old and did look pale and listless. While the summer months give plenty of fresh air and exercise, the diet is a monotonous repetition of *chapati*, made from flour carried up the mountain, washed down with endless cups of *Nun chai* or Kashmiri tea – a reddish liquid made from handfuls of green tea, a little soda and a lot of salt and goat's milk. Both are delicious after a long day's walk, but not a very balanced diet for months on end. In the end I gave her a supply of vitamin pills which usually seemed the best "medicine" to distribute.

"This was the first time the pass had been crossed for thirteen years"

Each summer shepherds come up with their goats to their own nai or meadow. They know every step of the way to their own grazing place (however many days' walk it is) but seldom travel from nai to nai. Walking for pleasure is a luxury of the rich. When we said we were thinking of going over the pass to Vishnesar the shepherd's first response was "impossible". We had expected this and, several cups of *nun chai* later, the impossible had become merely a strange thing to do. As time went on the adventure began to appeal to him and he volunteered to come with us. We set off the next morning, five of us instead of four.

Although nowhere near "impossible" it proved a very hard walk; a long slog across a permanently frozen glacier followed by a sustained and strenuous rock scramble. It was longer still for the ponies who could not scramble but had to toil up in endless diagonal lines. A few eagles made sudden black shadows; two marmots whistled to each other standing up on their hind legs; a lone bear lurched away in the distance. By the time we reached the top of the pass the sky was midday blue and deep copper-coloured rocks made jagged silhouettes against it. We collapsed on the summit before starting the deep descent. Calculating for a minute, the shepherd announced with indisputable authority that this was the first time the pass had been crossed for thirteen years and the first time ever that it had been crossed by ponies. He said it had no name so we called it Manikar pass. The achievement of a pass which was new to all of us cemented the sense of solidarity between Rashid, the pony men and myself.

LIZ MAUDSLAY

AFTER READING

1 Pick out three sentences or phrases which suggest that this is a personal account.

2 How would you describe Liz Maudslay's attitude to the people and places she sees?

COMPARE

Discussion

1   The holiday brochure uses many adjectives to describe the journey it is selling, such as *dramatic*, *astonishing* and *magnificent*. In pairs, find five more, then pick out five adjectives from Liz Maudslay's text, and comment on any differences you notice.

2   What are the advantages and disadvantages of seeing a country through a structured vacation rather than as a lone traveller? Organise a classroom debate with some of you taking the roles of travellers like Liz Maudslay, and others playing representatives from a travel company.

Assignments

1   Choose three or four paragraphs from Liz Maudslay's account and rewrite them for a holiday brochure. Then write a paragraph explaining what you changed – words, vocabulary, style and tone.

2   Using the kind of language in the holiday brochure, write the text for a three-day visit to your area. Then, for contrast, write a traveller's account of exploring the same place. Try to keep the tone of both assignments as serious as possible.

3   *Real travel means going it alone, not being part of a package tour arranged by someone else. Real travel means taking risks and cannot be organised in advance.*
How far do you agree? Write an essay, based on your own reading and experiences which examines the nature of 'real' travel.

THE SEA'S MERCY

■ However much technology has improved our ability to travel in comfort, sea travel remains terrifying for many people; we remain at the mercy of the powerful ocean. Compare these three accounts of sea travel.

1 Reread the passage aloud, emphasising its rhythm. Why is the rhythm significant?

2 What, in a sentence, is the psalm saying about the sea?

Psalm 107

They that go down to the sea in ships, that do business in
    great waters;
These see the works of the Lord, and his wonders
    in the deep.
For he commandeth, and raiseth the stormy wind, which
    lifteth up the waves thereof.
They mount up to the heaven, they go down again to the
    depths; their soul is melted because of trouble.
They reel to and fro, and stagger like a drunken man, and
    are at their wit's end.
Then they cry unto the Lord in their trouble, and he
    bringeth them out of their distresses.
He maketh the storm a calm, so that the waves thereof
    are still.
Then are they glad because they be quiet; so he bringeth
    them unto their desired haven.

VERSES 23-30
THE AUTHORIZED VERSION

Journal, 1849

Saturday Oct 13

Rose early this morning, opened my bulls eye window, & looked out to the East. The sun was just rising, the horizon was red; a familiar sight to me, reminding me of old times. Before breakfast went up to the mast-head, by way of gymnastics. About 10 o'clock a.m. the wind rose, the rain fell, & the deck looked dismally enough. By dinner time, it blew half a gale, & the passengers mostly retired to their rooms, sea sick. After dinner, the rain ceased, yet it still blew stiffly, & we were slowly forging along under close-reefed topsails – mainsail furled. I was walking the deck, when I perceived one of the steerage passengers looking over the side; I looked too, & saw a man in the water, his head completely lifted above the water - about twelve feet from the ship, right abreast the gangway. For an instant, I thought I was dreaming; for no one seemed to see what I did. Next moment, I shouted 'Man overboard!' & turned to go aft. The Captain ran forward, greatly confused. I dropped overboard the tackle-fall of the quarter-boat, & swung it towards the man, who was now drifting close to the ship. He did not get hold of it, & I got over the side, within a foot or two of the sea, & again swung the rope towards him. He now got hold of it. By this time, a crowd of people – sailors and others – were clustering about the bulwarks; but none seemed very anxious to save him. They warned *me* however, not to fall overboard. After holding on to the rope, about a quarter of a minute the man let go of it, & drifted astern under the mizzen chains. Four or five of the seamen jumped over into the chains & swung him more ropes. But his conduct was unaccountable; he could have saved himself, had he been so minded. I was struck by the expression of his face in the water. It was merry. At last he drifted off under the ship's counter, & all hands cried 'He's gone!' Running to the taffrail, we saw him again, floating off – saw a few bubbles, & never saw him again. No boat was lowered, no sail was shortened, hardly any noise was made.

The man drowned like a bullock. It afterwards turned out that he was crazy, & had jumped overboard. He had declared he would do so several times; & just before he did jump, he had tried to get possession of his child, in order to jump into the sea, with the child in his arms. His wife was miserably sick in her berth. The Captain said that this was the fourth or fifth instance he had known of people jumping overboard. He told a story of a man who did so, with his wife on deck at the time. As they were trying to save him, the wife said it was no use; & when he was drowned, she said 'there were plenty more men to be had'. Amiable creature! – By night, it blew a terrific gale, & we hove to. Miserable time! nearly every one sick, & the ship rolling & pitching in an amazing manner. About midnight, I rose & went on deck. It was blowing horribly – pitch dark, & raining. The Captain was in the cuddy & directed my attention 'to those fellows' as he called them meaning several 'Corposant balls' on the yard arms & mast heads. They were the first I had ever seen, & resembled large, dim stars in the sky.

HERMAN MELVILLE

AFTER READING

1 What is Herman Melville's attitude to the events he witnesses?

2 Which words show that the extract was written long ago? Are there any other clues?

The Shipwreck

'All hands unmoor!' proclaims a boisterous cry:
'All hands unmoor,' the cavern'd rocks reply!
Rous'd from repose, aloft the sailors swarm,
And with their levers soon the windlass arm.
The order given, up-springing with a bound,
They lodge the bars, and wheel their engine round:
At every turn the clanging pauls resound:
Uptorn reluctant from its oozy cave,
The ponderous anchor rises o'er the wave.
Along their slippery masts the yards ascend,
And high in air, the canvas wings extend:
Redoubling cords the lofty canvas guide,
And thro' inextricable mazes glide.
The lunar rays with long reflection gleam,
To light the vessel o'er the silver stream:
Along the glassy plane serene she glides,

While azure radiance trembles on her sides.
From east to north the transient breezes play;
And in th'Egyptian quarter soon decay.
A calm ensues; they dread th'adjacent shore;
The boats with rowers arm'd are sent before:
With cordage fasten'd to the lofty prow,
Aloof to sea the stately ship they tow.

When from the left approaching they descry
A liquid column towering shoot on high.
The foaming base an angry whirlwind sweeps,
Where curling billows rouse the fearful deeps.
Still round and round the fluid vortex flies,
Scattering dun night and horror thro' the skies,
The swift volution and th'enormous train
Let sages vers'd in nature's lore explain!
The horrid apparition still draws nigh,
And white with foam the whirling surges fly!
The guns were prim'd; the vessel northward veers
Till her black battery on the column bears.
The nitre fir'd; and while the dreadful sound,
Convulsive, shook the slumbering air around,
The watry volume, trembling to the sky,
Burst down a dreadful deluge from on high!
Th'affrighted surge, recoiling as it fell,
Rolling in hills disclos'd th'abyss of hell.
But soon, this transient undulation o'er,
The sea subsides; the whirlwinds rage no more.

For, while with boundless inundation o'er
The sea-beat ship th'involving waters roar,
Displaced beneath by her capacious womb,
They rage, their ancient station to resume;
By secret ambushes, their force to prove,
Thro' many a winding channel first they rove;
Till, gathering fury, like the fever'd blood,
Thro' her dark veins they roll a rapid flood.
While unrelenting thus the leaks they found,
The pumps with ever-clanking strokes resound.
Around each leaping valve, by toil subdu'd,
The tough bull-hide must ever be renew'd.

'Starboard again!' the watchful pilot cries;
'Starboard,' th'obedient timoneer replies.
Then to the left the ruling helm returns;
The wheel revolves; the ringing axle burns!
The ship no longer, foundering by the lee,
Bears on her side th'invasions of the sea:
All lonely o'er the desert waste she flies,
Scourged on by surges, storm and bursting skies.
As when the masters of the lance assail,
In Hyperborean seas, the slumbering whale;
Soon as the javelins pierce his scaly hide,
With anguish stung, he cleaves the downward tide.
In vain he flies, no friendly respite found;
His life-blood gushes thro' th'inflaming wound.

The wounded bark, thus smarting with her pain,
Scuds from pursuing waves along the main;
While, dash'd apart by her dividing prow,
Like burning adamant the waters glow.
Her joints forget their firm elastic tone;
Her long keel trembles, and her timbers groan.
Upheaved behind her, in tremendous height,
The billows frown, with fearful radiance bright!
Now shivering, o'er the topmost wave she rides,
While, deep beneath th'enormous gulf divides.
Now, launching headlong down the horrid vale,
She hears no more the roaring of the gale;
Till up the dreadful height again she flies,
Trembling beneath the current of the skies.

WILLIAM FALCONER

AFTER READING

1 In groups, prepare a choral reading of the poem, making it as dramatic as possible.

2 Summarise, in two or three points, what happens in the poem.

3 Does this extract treat storms at sea in a light-hearted or a serious way? Give an example to support your opinion.

COMPARE

Discussion

1 In pairs discuss which of the three extracts:

- gives the strongest impression of terror at sea
- is easiest to understand
- shows the writer's attitude most clearly
- seems least concerned
- seems oldest

For each answer, find an example to support your ideas.

2 Discuss the impression of the sea given by the two poetic texts – what advantages and disadvantages does the poetic form have in describing the power of the sea?

Assignments

1 Take the storyline of William Falconer's poem and rewrite it as a journal account like Herman Melville's. Try to keep some of the original language of the poem in your new version.

2 How do the writers suggest the power of the sea? Look, for example, at the psalm's simile 'stagger like a drunken man'. What image does this create? From each text pick out two or three examples which illustrate the force of the ocean, and write a paragraph about each, explaining its effect.

3 Write about the theme of the sea. What is it that causes such a mixture of fascination, awe and fear? Use any of your own experiences or reading memories to write about your own response - either as fact or fiction.

THE END OF THE EARTH

■ Few parts of the Earth remain as wildernesses. Compare these two accounts of journeys to the Poles – one to the South made in 1912 by Captain Robert Scott, the other to the North in 1989 by a team led by Robert Swan.

An Awful Place

Wednesday, January 18, 1912

...Great God! This is an awful place and terrible enough for us to have laboured to it without the reward of priority....

Now for the run home and a desperate struggle. I wonder if we can do it.

Friday, March 16 or Saturday 17

Lost track of dates, but think the last correct. Tragedy all along the line. At lunch, the day before yesterday, poor Titus Oates said he couldn't go on; he proposed we should leave him in his sleeping-bag. That we could not do, and we induced him to come on, on the afternoon march. In spite of its awful nature for him he struggled on and we made a few miles. At night he was worse and we knew the end had come....

...This was the end. He slept through the night before last, hoping not to wake; but he woke in the morning – yesterday. It was blowing a blizzard. He said, 'I am just going outside and may be some time.' He went out into the blizzard and we have not seen him since....

Monday, March 19

Lunch. We camped with difficulty last night, and were dreadfully cold till after our supper of cold pemmican and biscuit and a half of pannikin of cocoa cooked over the spirit. Then, contrary to expectation, we got warm and all slept well. To-day we started in the usual dragging manner. Sledge dreadfully heavy. We are 15 ½ miles from the depôt and out to get there in three days. What progress! We have two days' food but barely a day's fuel. All our feet are getting bad – Wilson's best, my right foot worst, left all right. There is no chance to nurse one's feet till we can get hot food into us. Amputation is the least I can hope for now, but will the trouble spread? That is the serious question. The weather doesn't give us a chance – the wind from N. to N.W. and -40° temp. to-day.

Wednesday, March 21

Got within 11 miles of depôt Monday night; had to lay up all yesterday in severe blizzard. To-day forlorn hope, Wilson and Bowers going to depôt for fuel.

Thursday, March 22 and 23

Blizzard bad as ever – Wilson and Bowers unable to start – to-morrow last chance – no fuel and only one or two of food left must be near the end. Have decided it shall be natural – we shall march for the depôt with or without our effects and die in our tracks.

Thursday, March 29

Since the 21st we have had a continuous gale from W.S.W. and S.W.

We had fuel to make two cups of tea apiece and bare food for two days on the 20th. Every day we have been ready to start for our depôt *11 miles* away, but outside the door of the tent it remains a scene of whirling drift. I do not think we can hope for any better things now. We shall stick it out to the end, but we are getting weaker, of course, and the end cannot be far. It seems a pity, but I do not think I can write more.

R. SCOTT

Last Entry

For God's sake look after our people.

ROBERT FALCON SCOTT

AFTER READING

1 Which word best describes the tone of Scott's journal: exhausted, bitter, terrified, desperate, pessimistic? Choose an example to support your opinion.

2 How would you describe the writer's attitude to his companions?

■ Robert Swan's expedition is more successful, but also fraught with problems.

Icewalk

WEEK 3 (APRIL 3-10)

One hundred miles down; three hundred to go. Six feet below, the ocean – a dark, still menace – groans, slowly shifting and cracking the ice...

Frostbite is all about. Darryl's feet are frostbitten and blistered; he is limping now. Arved's face is peeling off in great chunks while Hiro's cheek is scorched. Gus is an excellent, hard man; a true Inuit in his element at long last...
The horizon spread before us like a rumpled white sheet and I thought again of Antarctica...

We scurried our way across gaps of water that opened wider as we crossed. It's like running the Grand National...

We have bundled up the scientific and medical samples ready for their journey to laboratories around the world. Rupert's haul includes great blocks of snow destined for the University of Hawaii!

WEEK 4 (April 10-17)

There has been no radio contact with base for three days now. Graeme has exhausted the radio batteries in a vain effort to attract the attention of the outside world...

More than one third of the journey lies behind us. Conditions are appalling. We had expected the pressure ridges to ease off at this latitude but instead we battle 10 to 12 hours a day sometimes making only five miles. We should be averaging at least 10...

Huddled around a coughing stove, rubbing our aching feet we are often too numb to talk, to think and to dream.

WEEK 5 (APRIL 17 – 24)

I had lost my spoon, Misha his balaclava. Minor incidents in the explorer's almanac of calamities, but inconvenient nevertheless. Misha found the balaclava on his head and, at the end of a day's uncomfortable travel, I found the spoon in my boot. I knew then we were exhausted...

Monday (April 17) and we are waiting to be found. The Argos satellite beacon had been transmitting since morning to allow the aircraft to locate us. The week had been hell, almost no radio contact, an unseasonable cold snap and, like Armundsen decades before us, an encounter with the Devil's Cauldron. It was as he described – an ocean frozen mid-storm, the ice caught in a perpetual and ferocious turbulence...

The Arctic prises the smallest problem wide open; it searches for our weaknesses and deftly takes advantage of them. My back has bothered me all my life but never more so than in this damned place.

WEEK 6 (APRIL 24-MAY 1)
So the race for the Pole gathers momentum. Having hit flatter ice last week we continue to slog 12 hours a day, marching at least 10...

We camp and attempt to locate some smooth ice for the resupply aircraft, delayed once again by bad weather. Our radios are down and we have had only scant contact with Advance Base Camp at Cape Aldrich these last few days...

Misha and I surge ahead at the close of each day's march and watch the men 'finish'. There ain't nothing or nobody who could stop the men at this point. Their heads are low as they wrestle to a halt. They are grimly determined; their bodies frozen but for the mechanical movements of their arms and legs. Ice coats their faces; they stop unable to move for a moment; comically bedraggled.

ROBERT SWAN

AFTER READING

1 Which word best describes the tone of Robert Swan's journal: excited, bitter, terrified, fascinated, heroic, optimistic? Choose an example to support your opinion.

2 How would you describe the writer's attitude to his companions?

COMPARE

Discussion

1 In pairs, decide which extract is:

- more personal
- more emotional
- more factual
- more descriptive
- more vivid.

Choose examples to support your choices.

2 Discuss which extract tells us more about the physical environment, and which tells us more about the writer.

3 Which extract do you find more interesting, and why?

Assignments

1 Take Captain Scott's diary extract and write a thirty-second radio news report announcing that the expedition has been lost. Use pieces of information from the diary to make your report as factual as possible.

2 Write your own diary account of a journey – however small – making it as factually accurate as possible. It might only be your daily journey to school – but try to give a strong sense of the people and places you see.

3 Write a comparison of the two diary extracts included here, looking in particular at the way the writers' personalities are revealed in the language they use. Compare their use of descriptive words, their attitudes to others, and their portrayal of themselves.

WIDER READING

Travel-writing Anthologies

Granta Books, *The Best of Granta Travel*; Jonathan Raban, *The Oxford Book of the Sea*; Geoff Barton, *Travel Writing*; Eric Newby, *A Book of Traveller's Tales*; Clive Brooks, *Life on the Liners*; Davies and Jansz, *Women Travel: Adventures, Advice and Experience*.

Travel Fiction

E M Forster, *A Room with a View*; Jules Verne, *Around the World in Eighty Days*; Paul Theroux, *The Mosquito Coast*; William Golding, *Rites of Passage, Close Quarters*, and *Fire Down Below*; Beryl Bainbridge, *The Goodbye Boys*; David Lodge, *Paradise News*.

1 Write a personal essay about the attraction of reading travel writing – what is its appeal compared with reading fiction?

2 Compare a real-life account of travel with a fictional narrative – for example, Captain Scott's diaries with Beryl Bainbridge's *The Goodbye Boys*.

3 Look at Jonathan Raban's anthology, *The Oxford Book of the Sea*. Choose four or five pieces of writing that you particularly enjoyed, and write an introduction to them for a new reader.

4 Compile your own anthology of travel writing, and write an introduction explaining your selections.

WORD POWER

Words are rarely neutral. We use them to label people and objects, to describe, to argue, to reveal our emotions. The words we use will vary according to where and when we are speaking, and who we are speaking to.

- *How do the words you use vary when addressing a stranger, your parents or your friends?*
- *How far do you think it is true that people are judged by their language — by their words and their pronunciation? Is this fair, or is it a form of prejudice?*

CHOOSING NAMES

■ One of the first decisions made for us by our parents is what we shall be called. We are more or less stuck with these names for the rest of our lives. We can shorten them, or take a nickname, or even change the names completely if we're very unhappy about them. But in general, names stick! What patterns are there in names? What names do we choose for pets; how are trade names chosen?

READING SKILLS
Scanning/skimming
Analysing language

Popular dog names

The list below shows the one hundred most frequently used names for dogs in the USA, as revealed by a computer-based study of some 25,000 dog licences.

1	Lady	24	Mitzie	47	Caesar
2	King	25	Tiger	48	Boots
3	Duke	26	Smokey	49	Kelly
4	Peppy	27	Charlie	50	Buttons
5	Prince	28	Chico		Tina
6	Pepper	29	Brandy	52	Sparky
7	Snoopy	30	Sheba	53	Daisy
8	Princess	31	Fluffy	54	Gigi
9	Heidi	32	Missy		Nicky
10	Sam		Toby	56	Spot
	Coco	34	Lucky	57	Gypsy
12	Butch		Trixie		Taffy
13	Penny	36	Mickey	59	Tuffy
14	Rusty	37	Tammy	60	Corky
15	Sandy	38	Cindy		Skipper
	Susie	39	Pierre	62	Misty
17	Duchess	40	Tiny		Frisky
18	Blackie	41	Max	64	Cookie
19	Ginger	42	Skippy	65	Buster
20	Queenie	43	Fifi		Dusty
21	Rex	44	Champ		Muffin
22	Candy	45	Fitz	68	Buddy
23	Buffy	46	Brownie		Teddy

1 Skim through the list and pick out the three names which you find least and most appropriate.

2 Skim again and spot how many dog names are also used for humans. What conclusions can be drawn from this?

70	Bruno	81	Scottie		Rags
71	Barney	82	Bridget	93	Brutus
72	Sassy		Lassie		Bullet
73	Bobo	84	Baby		Samson
	Joe		Jack		Shadow
	Mike	86	Midnight	97	Dolly
76	Rocky		Patches		Gretchen
77	Snowball		Poncho	99	Pal
78	Benji	89	Happy	100	Maggie
	Peanuts	90	Jojo		
80	Laddie		Mac		

Popular cat names

A survey of British cat names, commissioned by Spillers Top Cat and carried out by the British Market Research Bureau, revealed the following most popular names:

1	Sooty	17	Ginger	33	Bumble		Purdy
2	Smokie		Lucy		Cindy		Sammy
3	Brandy		Tim		Daisy		Scamp
	Fluffy		Tiny		Dusty		Shandy
	Tiger	21	Charlie		Fred		Sherry
6	Tibbie		Lucky		Frisky		Simon
	Tiggie		Rusty		Honey		Tabitha
	Tom		Snowy		Jerry		Topsy
9	Kitty	25	Candy		Katie		Twiggy
	Sam		Cat		Kizzy		
	Sandy		Flossie		Mickey		
	Tinker		Mitzi		Nelson		
13	Blackie		Puss		Oliver		
	Susie		Sally		Penny		
	Toby		Sukie		Pepper		
	Whisky		Tammy		Pickles		

1 Again, skim through the list and pick out the three names which you find least and most appropriate.

2 Skim again and spot how many cat names are also used for humans – about what proportion?

SPILLERS FOODS

Trade names

*Look at the following list of product names and the
explanations of where the names came from.*

Adidas a company founded by Adolf Dassler (1900-78)
known to his friends as Adi. He added the first
three lettters of his last name to form the trade
name.

Aspirin from German *acetylirte spirsäure* ('acetylated
spiraeic acid') plus the chemical suffix *-in*.

Babycham originally for the 'baby chamois' used as an
emblem, though a link with 'champagne' was
inevitable in the minds of customers.

Bejam from the initials of Brian (brother), Eric (father)
and John Apthorp (founder of the company), and
Millie and Marion (mother and sister).

Calor gas Calor is Latin for 'heat'.

C & A founded by the Dutch brothers Clemens and
August Brenninkmeyer.

Drambuie from Gaelic *dram* 'drink' and *buidh* 'yellow'.

Fanta from the German word *fantasie* 'fantasia'.

Harpic the inventor was Harry Pickup.

Hovis suggested in a competition to find a suitable
trade name by Herbert Grime in 1890. He based
it on Latin *hominis vis* 'strength of man'.

Kia-Ora Maori 'good health'.

Lego Danish *leg godt* 'play well'.

Meccano from the phrase 'mechanics made easy'.

Nivea the feminine of Latin *niveus* 'snowy'.

Ovaltine originally 'Ovomaltine' from Latin *ovum* 'egg',
'malt' and *-ine*. Shortened to Ovaltine when
introduced to Britain from Switzerland.

Pepsi Cola influenced by Coca Cola and intended to relieve
dyspepsia [indigestion].

Perspex Latin *perspexi* 'I looked through'.

Quink from 'quick-drying ink'.

Ribena the Latin botanical term for the blackcurrant is
Ribes nigrum, which suggested this name.

Sony	based on Latin *son* 'sound'.
Tesco	founded by Sir John Cohen, one of whose earliest suppliers was T E Stockwell. The latter's initials plus the first two letters of Cohen led to Tesco.
Volvo	Latin 'I roll'.
Wimpy	J Wellington Wimpy was a hamburger-loving character in the Popeye cartoon strips.

ADRIAN ROOM
NTC'S Dictionary of Trade Name Origins

AFTER READING

1 Skim through the list and pick out the three names which you find least and most appropriate.

2 Think of any other famous product and make a guess at why the name was chosen.

COMPARE

Discussion

1 In pairs, look for any patterns of sounds or spellings in the dog and cat names, particularly the endings of these words. What patterns do you find and how can you explain them? Then do the same for the trade names.

2 Try to group the pet names according to areas of meaning (sometimes called 'semantic fields'); for example: colour (Blackie), movement (Skippy), and so on. How many other semantic fields can you find? What semantic fields can you find for the trade names?

3 Make a comparison of the semantic fields used for dogs and cats – are there any obvious differences in the types of names used?

Assignments

1 Choose a product – such as chocolate bars or soft drinks – and make a list of all the product names you can think of. Then write a brief description of why the names might have been chosen and what they are supposed to suggest. What do you notice about the spellings? Is there a difference between the names of products intended for young consumers, and those for older people?

2 Have a look through a weekend newspaper and make a list of some of the names given to racehorses. Write an analysis of these names according to spelling, sound and semantic fields.

3 Think of any creatures for which you have chosen names – cats, dogs, hamsters, goldfish. What names did you choose? How did you decide on them? What kinds of names would you not have chosen? Write a brief personal essay reflecting on the decision-making process you used in choosing names.

WORDS OF LOVE

■ It has been said that it is impossible to be original when we're in love – all we can say is 'I love you'. Compare these four love poems from different ages and countries, and examine the ways in which their authors express their feelings. The first was written in the nineteenth century.

READING SKILLS

Reading aloud

Studying genre

AFTER READING

1 What is the main message of this poem?

2 On a scale of 1 (least) to 5 (most), how personal is this poem?

Sonnet from the Portuguese

How do I love thee? Let me count the ways.

I love thee to the depth and breadth and height

My soul can reach, when feeling out of sight

For the ends of Being and ideal Grace.

I love thee to the level of everyday's

Most quiet need, by sun and candlelight.

I love thee freely, as men strive for Right;

I love thee purely, as they turn from Praise.

I love thee with the passion put to use

In my old griefs, and with my childhood's faith.

I love thee with a love I seemed to lose

With my lost saints – I love thee with the breath,

Smiles, tears, of all my life! – and, if God choose,

I shall but love thee better after death.

ELIZABETH BARRETT BROWNING

■ This sonnet was written by an American in the first half of the twentieth century.

AFTER READING

1 What is the main message of this poem?

2 On a scale of 1 (least) to 5 (most), how personal is this poem?

■ This love poem has been translated from the original Chinese.

What lips my lips have kissed

What lips my lips have kissed, and where, and why,
I have forgotten, and what arms have lain
Under my head till morning; but the rain
Is full of ghosts tonight, that tap and sigh
Upon the glass and listen for reply,
And in my heart there stirs a quiet pain
For unremembered lads that not again
Will turn to me at midnight with a cry.
Thus in the winter stands the lonely tree,
Nor knows what birds have vanished one by one,
Yet knows its boughs more silent than before:
I cannot say what loves have come and gone,
I only know that summer sang in me
A little while, that in me sings no more.

EDNA ST VINCENT MILLAY

Untitled

I slipped down the terrace, watching you leave
By the small leafy path.
Wait! Are you going far, very far?
I dashed down, stopping in front of you.
'Are you scared?'
Silently I caress the button on your jacket.
Yes, I am scared.
But I won't tell you why.

We strolled around the river bend.
The night, though soothing, moved us.
Arm in arm we walked along the bank,
Threading in and out of the cinnamon trees.
'Are you happy?'

Looking up, I find stars swarming towards me.
Yes, I am happy.
But I won't tell you why.

You bent over the desk,
Discovering the awkward lines I wrote.
Blushing deeply I snatched up my poems.
Solemnly, tenderly you blessed me.
'Ah, you are in love.'
I secretly sigh.
Yes, I am in love,
But I won't tell you why.

SHU TING

A GENTLE REQUIEM

Images of your face
Bring me
The wild mane of summer leaves
And the sound of creepers on windows.

Terror is you in the distance
The wind on mad waters
The smell of incense in abattoirs
Brushing sleep into unclean corners.

Gyrating dreams weave on time
Designs of chaos.
Ice throttles silence: air animates rust.
Beneath water fire-shells survive.

Then sometimes in deep weather a door bursts open:
Lights thread the shadow
Waters run riot, and the colours of death
Crystallise lions in panic.

Beneath pain fire-dreams revive.
Waves rush over glass
Leaving only a ripple
On your face.

BEN OKRI

■ This poem was written in English by an African writer.

COMPARE

Discussion

1 Which of the poems is:

- most romantic
- most dramatic
- most intimate
- easiest to follow?

For each decision you make, be prepared to provide evidence.

2 Discuss the different techniques the poets use to express their feelings, grouping them according to these headings:

- using statements
- using argument
- writing about the self
- writing about the other person
- using images of nature
- using images of death
- using very poetic language
- using everyday language

3 In pairs, choose one of the poems and prepare a reading in two different styles – one obviously romantic, one very matter-of-fact. How does the poem's meaning change when the style of reading it aloud differs?

4 'Untitled' is the only translated poem. Compare it to the other poems – how far can you tell that it has been translated? Does it retain any of its Chinese feel?

Assignments

1 Choose one of the poems and try to write the lover's reply. Try to imitate the original structure of the poem. Then write a paragraph discussing what you think worked/didn't work, and any problems you encountered.

2 Copy out the lyrics of a recent song about love, and write an essay about the way the writer expresses him or herself. What techniques are used? How poetic is the language? How well does the music fit with the lyrics? How could the language of the song have been improved?

3 Compile your own anthology of five to ten love poems and write an introduction to them, explaining why you chose them, what you like about them, how the writers express their feelings, and anything unusual or distinctive that you notice about the language.

USE AND MISUSE ≡≡≡

■ Language is frequently controversial, provoking arguments about the way it is used. English is a complex and varied language, and can be used to conceal as well as to express meanings. The first of these two extracts examines the idiosyncrasies of our Mother Tongue.

READING SKILLS

Summarising

Seeking information

Analysing language

MOTHER TONGUE

If you have a morbid fear of peanut butter sticking to the roof of your mouth, there is a word for it: *arachibutyrophobia*. There is a word to describe the state of being a woman: *muliebrity*. And there's a word for describing a sudden breaking off of thought: *aposiopesis*. If you harbour an urge to look through the windows of the homes you pass, there is a word for the condition: *crytoscopophilia*. When you are just dropping off to sleep and you experience that sudden sensation of falling, there is a word for it: it's a *myoclonic jerk*.... In English, in short, there are words for almost everything.

Some of these words deserve to be better known. Take *velleity*, which describes a mild desire, a wish or urge too slight to lead to action. Doesn't that seem a useful term? Or how about *slubberdegullion*, a seventeenth-century word signifying a worthless or slovenly fellow? Or *ugsome*, a late medieval word meaning loathsome or disgusting? It has lasted half a millennium in English, was a common synonym for *horrid* until well into the last century, and can still be found tucked away forgotten at the back of most unabridged dictionaries. Isn't it a shame to let it slip away? Our dictionaries are full of such words – words describing the most specific of conditions, the most improbable of contingencies, the most arcane of distinctions.

And yet there are odd gaps. We have no word for coolness corresponding to warmth. We are strangely lacking in middling terms – words to describe with some precision the middle ground between hard and soft, near and far, big and little. We have a possessive impersonal pronoun *its* to place alongside *his*, *her* and *their* but no equivalent impersonal pronoun to contrast with the personal *whose*. Thus we have to rely on inelegant constructions such as 'the house whose roof' or resort to periphrasis. We have a word to describe all the work you find waiting for you when you return from vacation, *backlog*, but none to describe all the work you have to do before you go. Why not *forelog*? And we have a large number of negative words – *inept*, *dishevelled*, *incorrigible*, *ruthless*, *unkempt* – for which the positive form is missing. English would be richer if we could say admiringly of a tidy person, 'She's *so* shevelled', or praise a capable person for being full of ept or and energetic one for having heaps of ert. Many of these words did once have positive forms. *Ruthless* was companioned by *ruth*, meaning compassion. One of Milton's poems contains the well-known line, 'Look homeward, Angel, now, and melt with ruth'. But, as with many such words, one form died and another lived. Why this should be is beyond explanation. Why should we have lose *demit* (send away) but saved *commit*? Why should *impede* have survived while the once equally common and seemingly just as useful *expede* expired? No one can say.

Despite these gaps and casualties, English retains probably the richest vocabulary, and most diverse shading of meanings, of any language. We can distinguish between house and home (as, for instance, the French cannot), between continual and continuous, sensual and sensuous, forceful and forcible, childish and childlike, masterly and masterful, assignment and assignation, informant and informer. For almost every word we have a multiplicity of synonyms. Something is not just big, it is large, immense, vast, capacious, bulky, massive, whopping. No other language has so many words all saying the same thing. It has been said that English is unique in possessing a synonym for each level of our culture: popular, literary, and scholarly – so that we can, according to our background and cerebral attainments, rise, mount, or ascend a stairway, shrink in fear, terror, or trepidation, and think, ponder, or cogitate upon a problem. This abundance of terms is often cited as a virtue. And yet a critic could equally argue that English is an untidy and acquisitive language, cluttered with a plethora of needless words. After all, do we really need *fictile* as a synonym for *mouldable*, *glabrous* for *hairless*, *sternutation* for *sneezing*? Jules Feiffer once drew a strip cartoon in which the down-at-heel character observed that first he was called poor, then needy, then deprived, then underprivileged, and then disadvantaged, and concluded that although he still didn't have a dime he sure had acquired a fine vocabulary. There is something in that. A rich vocabulary carries with it a concomitant danger of verbosity, as evidenced by our peculiar affection for redundant phrases, expressions that say the same thing twice: *beck and call, law and order, assault and battery, null and void, safe and sound, first and foremost, trials and tribulations, hem and haw, spick-and-span, kith and kin, dig and delve, hale and hearty, peace and quiet, vim and vigour, pots and pans, cease and desist, rack and ruin, without let or hindrance, to all intents and purposes, various different*.

Despite this bounty of terms, we have a strange – and to foreigners it must seem maddening – tendency to load a single word with a whole galaxy of meanings. *Fine*, for instance, has fourteen definitions as an adjective, six as a noun and two as an adverb. In the *Oxford English Dictionary* it fills two full pages and takes 5,000 words of description. We can talk about fine art, fine gold, a fine edge, feeling fine, fine hair, and a court fine and mean quite separate things. The condition of having many meanings is known as *polysemy*, and it is very common. *Sound* is another polysemic word. Its vast repertory of meanings can suggest an audible noise, a state of healthiness (sound mind), an outburst (sound off), an inquiry (sound out), a body of water (Puget Sound), or financial stability (sound economy), among many others. And then there's *round*. In the *OED*, *round* alone (that is without variations like *rounded* and *roundup*) takes 7½ pages to define, or about 15,000 words of text – about as much as is contained in the first forty pages of this book. Even when you strip out its obsolete senses, *round* still has twelve uses as an adjective, nineteen as a noun, seven as a transitive verb, five as an intransitive verb, one as an adverb, and two as a preposition. But the polysemic champion must be *set*. Superficially it looks a wholly unassuming monosyllable, the verbal equivalent of the single-celled organism. Yet is has 58 uses as a noun, 126 as a verb, and 10 as a participle adjective. Its meanings are so various and scattered that it takes the *OED* 60,000 words – the length of a short novel – to discuss them all. A foreigner could be excused for thinking that to know *set* is to know English.

BILL BRYSON

AFTER READING

1 List three points that Bill Bryson is making in this extract.

2 In what ways does the extract show that English differs from other languages?

■ This extract, written by an American, shows how language can be used to mislead and deceive.

THE WORLD OF DOUBLESPEAK

*F*armers no longer have cows, pigs, chickens, or other animals on their farms; according to the US Department of Agriculture farmers have 'grain-consuming animal units' (which, according to the Tax Reform Act of 1986, are kept in 'single-purpose agricultural structures,' not pig pens and chicken coops). Attentive observers of the English language also learned recently that the multibillion-dollar stock market crash of 1987 was simply a 'fourth quarter equity retreat'; that airplanes don't crash, they just have 'uncontrolled contact with the ground'; that janitors are really 'environmental technicians'; that it was a 'diagnostic misadventure of a high magnitude' which caused the death of a patient in a Philadelphia hospital, not medical malpractice; and that President Reagan wasn't really unconscious while he underwent minor surgery, he was just in a 'non-decision-making form.' In other words, doublespeak continues to spread as the official language of public discourse.

Doublespeak is a blanket term for language which pretends to communicate but doesn't, language which makes the bad seem good, the negative appear positive, the unpleasant attractive, or at least tolerable. It is language which avoids, shifts, or denies responsibility, language which is at variance with its real or its purported meaning. It is language which conceals or prevents thought. Basic to doublespeak is incongruity, the incongruity between what is said, or left unsaid, and what really is: between the word and the referent, between seem and be, between the essential function of language, communication, and what doublespeak does – mislead, distort, deceive, inflate, circumvent, obfuscate.

When shopping, we are asked to check our packages at the desk 'for our convenience,' when it's not for our convenience at all but for the store's 'program to reduce inventory shrinkage.' We see advertisements for 'preowned,' 'experienced,' or 'previously distinguished' cars, for 'genuine imitation leather,' 'virgin vinyl,' or 'real counterfeit diamonds.' Television offers not reruns but 'encore telecasts.' There are no slums or ghettos, just the 'inner city' or 'sub-standard housing' where the 'disadvantaged,' 'economically non-affluent,' or 'fiscal underachievers' live. Nonprofit organisations don't make a profit, they have 'negative deficits' or 'revenue excesses.' In the world of doublespeak dying is 'terminal living.'

We know that a toothbrush is still a toothbrush even if the advertisements on television call it a 'home plaque removal instrument,' and even that 'nutritional avoidance therapy' means a diet. But who would guess that a 'volume-related production schedule adjustment' means closing an entire factory in the doublespeak of General Motors, or that 'advanced downward adjustments' means budget cuts in the doublespeak of Caspar Weinberger, or that 'energetic disassembly' means an explosion in a nuclear power plant in the doublespeak of the nuclear power industry?

The euphemism, an inoffensive or positive word or phrase designed to avoid a harsh, unpleasant, or distasteful reality, can at times be doublespeak. But the euphemism can also be a tactful word or phrase; for example, 'passed away' functions not just to protect the feelings of another person but also to express our concern for another's grief. This use of the euphemism is not doublespeak but the language of courtesy. A euphemism used to mislead or deceive, however, becomes doublespeak. In 1984, the US State Department announced that in its annual reports on the status of human rights in countries around the world it would no longer use the word 'killing.' Instead, it would use the phrase 'unlawful or arbitrary deprivation of life.' Thus the State Department avoids discussing government-sanctioned killings in countries that the United States supports and has certified as respecting human rights.

The Pentagon also avoids unpleasant realities when it refers to bombs and artillery shells which fall on civilian targets as 'incontinent ordnance,' or killing the enemy as 'servicing the target.' In 1977 the Pentagon tried to slip funding for the neutron bomb unnoticed into an appropriations bill by calling it an 'enhanced radiation device.' And in 1971 the CIA gave us that most famous of examples of doublespeak when it used the phrase 'eliminate with extreme prejudice' to refer to the execution of a suspected double agent in Vietnam.

WILLIAM LUTZ

AFTER READING

1 List three points that William Lutz is making in this extract.

2 Based on your reading of this extract, give a definition of the terms DOUBLESPEAK and EUPHEMISM.

COMPARE

Discussion

1   Bill Bryson makes the point that in English there are often several words for more or less the same thing, e.g. *rise, mount, ascend.* Look at the list of words below. In pairs, think of as many words as you can which mean more or less the same as these:

- fast
- slow
- car
- frightening
- eat

Now, for one of the words, write down sentences which illustrate the small variations of meaning you have found.

2   William Lutz describes euphemisms – words which avoid saying something harsh or unpleasant. Make a list of euphemisms for these topics:

- death
- illness
- sadness

For each topic, place the words you have chosen on a scale of most to least formal to show when they might be used.

3   Discuss the advantages and disadvantages of having several words to mean the same thing, and of the existence of euphemisms. For each topic, do the advantages outweigh the disadvantages?

Assignments

1   Write a simple story (a couple of paragraphs) about someone's journey to work. Then, using a Thesaurus, rewrite the story with more complex vocabulary, making it deliberately verbose. Write a paragraph describing the effect of changing the vocabulary in this way.

2   Young people often use words that older people don't know. One group of Year 11 pupils, for example, put together a dictionary of the words they frequently use:

EFFECTIVE	*adj.* very good
ELEPHANTS	*n.* flares
NASH	*vb.* run; get away
NASTY	*adj.* **1.** beautiful **2.** not very nice at all
RABBA	*vb.* to foam violently at the mouth
RABID	*adj.* having rabies
RARF	*n.* annoying person
SHANN	*adj.* very poor
SMART	*adj.* most excellent; fashionable
SORTED	*adj.* **1.** correct **2.** most excellent **3.** thank you
YAFFERS	*n.* disproportionately large collar on item of clothing
YOFF	*vb.* laugh

Compile your own dictionary, setting it out like this one.

LESSONS IN PRONUNCIATION

■ In Bernard Shaw's play, first performed in 1914, Liza Doolittle, a London flower girl, visits Henry Higgins, an expert on pronunciation, and his friend Colonel Pickering. In groups of four read the following extract aloud.

READING SKILLS

Reading aloud

Analysing language

Pygmalion

HIGGINS	Tired of listening to sounds?
PICKERING	Yes. It's a fearful strain. I rather fancied myself because I can pronounce twenty-four distinct vowel sounds; but your hundred and thirty beat me. I can't hear a bit of difference between most of them.
HIGGINS	*(chuckling and going over to the piano to eat sweets)* Oh. that comes with practice. You hear no difference at first; but you keep on listening, and presently you find they're all as different as A from B. *(Mrs Pearce looks in: she is Higgins's housekeeper)*. What's the matter?
MRS PEARCE	*(hesitating, evidently perplexed)* A young woman asks to see you, sir.
HIGGINS	A young woman! What does she want?
MRS PEARCE	Well, sir, she says you'll be glad to see her when you know what she's come about. She's quite a common girl, sir. Very common indeed. I should have sent her away, only I thought perhaps you wanted her to talk into your machines. I hope I've not done wrong; but really you see such queer people sometimes – you'll excuse me, I'm sure sir –
HIGGINS	Oh, that's all right, Mrs Pearce. Has she an interesting accent?
MRS PEARCE	Oh, something dreadful, sir, really. I don't

know how you can take an interest in it.

HIGGINS   (to Pickering) Let's have her up. Shew her up, Mrs Pearce (he rushes across to his working table and picks out a cylinder to use on the phonograph.)

MRS PEARCE   (only half resigned to it) Very well, sir. It's for you to say. (She goes downstairs).

HIGGINS   This is rather a bit of luck. I'll shew you how I make records. We'll set her talking; and I'll take it down first in Bell's Visible Speech; then in broad Romic; and then we'll get her on the phonograph so that you can turn her on as often as you like with the written transcript before you.

MRS PEARCE   (returning) This is the young woman, sir.

from *My Fair Lady*, the musical adaptation of *Pygmalion*

The flower girl enters in state. She has a hat with three ostrich feathers, orange, sky-blue, and red. She has a nearly clean apron and the shoddy coat has been tidied a little. The pathos of this deplorable figure, with its innocent vanity and consequential air, touches Pickering, who has already straightened himself in the presence of Mrs Pearce. But as to Higgins, the only distinction he makes between men and women is that when he is neither bullying nor exclaiming to the heavens against some featherweight cross, he coaxes women as a child coaxes its nurse when it wants to get anything out of her.

HIGGINS   (brusquely, recognizing her with unconcealed disappointment, and at once, babylike, making an intolerable grievance of it)

Why, this is the girl I jotted down last night. She's no use: I've got all the records I want of the Lisson Grove lingo; and I'm not going to waste another cylinder on it. (To the girl) Be off with you: I don't want you.

THE FLOWER GIRL	Don't you be so saucy. You ain't heard what I come for yet. *(To Mrs Pearce, who is waiting at the door for further instructions)* Did you tell him I come in a taxi?
MRS PEARCE	Nonsense, girl! what do you think a gentleman like Mr Higgins cares what you came in?
THE FLOWER GIRL	Oh, we are proud! He ain't above giving lessons, not him: I heard him say so. Well, I ain't come here to ask for any compliment; and if my money's not good enough I can go elsewhere.
HIGGINS	Good enough for what?
THE FLOWER GIRL	Good enough for you. Now you know, don't you? I'm come to have lessons, I am. And to pay for 'em too: make no mistake.
HIGGINS	*(stupent)* Well!!! *(Recovering his breath with a gasp)* What do you expect me to say to you?
THE FLOWER GIRL	Well, if you was a gentleman, you might ask me to sit down, I think. Don't I tell you I'm bringing you business?
HIGGINS	Pickering: shall we ask this baggage to sit down, or shall we throw her out of the window?
THE FLOWER GIRL	*(running away in terror to the piano, where she turns at bay)* Ah-ah-oh-ow-ow-ow-oo! *(Wounded and whimpering)* I won't be called a baggage when I've offered to pay like any lady.

Motionless, the two men stare at her from the other side of the room, amazed.

PICKERING	*(gently)* But what is it you want?
THE FLOWER GIRL	I want to be a lady in a flower shop 'stead of sellin' at the corner of Tottenham Court Road. But they won't take me unless I can talk more genteel. He said he could teach

me. Well, here I am ready to pay him – not asking any favour and he treats me zif I was dirt.

MRS PEARCE   How can you be such a foolish ignorant girl as to think you could afford to pay Mr Higgins?

THE FLOWER GIRL   Why shouldn't I? I know what lessons cost as well as you do; and I'm ready to pay.

HIGGINS   How much?

THE FLOWER GIRL   *(coming back to him triumphant)* Now you're talking! I thought you'd come off it when you saw a chance of getting back a bit of what you chucked at me last night. *(Confidentially)* You'd had a drop in, hadn't you?

HIGGINS   *(peremptorily)* Sit down.

THE FLOWER GIRL   Oh, if you're going to make a compliment of it

HIGGINS   *(thundering at her)* Sit down, girl. Do as you're told.

THE FLOWER GIRL   Ah-ah-ah-ow-ow-oo! *(She stands, half rebellious, half bewildered)*

PICKERING   *(very courteous)* Won't you sit down? *(He places the stray chair near the hearthrug between himself and Higgins).*

THE FLOWER GIRL   *(coyly)* Don't mind if I do. *(She sits down. Pickering returns to the hearthrug)*

HIGGINS   What's your name?

THE FLOWER GIRL   Liza Doolittle

HIGGINS   *(declaiming gravely)*
Eliza, Elizabeth, Betsy and Bess.
They went to the woods to get a
    bird's nes':

PICKERING   They found a nest with four eggs in it.

HIGGINS   They took one apiece, and left three in it.

They laugh heartily at their own fun.

LIZA	Oh don't be silly.
MRS PEARCE	*(placing herself behind Liza's chair)* You mustn't speak to the gentleman like that.
LIZA	Well, why won't he speak sensible to me?
HIGGINS	Come back to business. How much do you propose to pay me for the lessons?
LIZA	Oh, I know what's right. A lady friend of mine gets French lessons for eighteen pence an hour from a real French gentleman. Well, you wouldn't have the face to ask me the same for teaching me my own language as you would for French: so I won't give no more than a shilling. Take it or leave it.

BERNARD SHAW

1 Summarise the events of the extract in one or two sentences.

2 How do you picture the setting for this scene? Make some brief notes or sketches.

Discussion

1 Make brief notes on what you notice about the characters of Higgins, Colonel Pickering, Mrs Pearce and Eliza Doolittle.

2 Now, having considered the characterisation in more detail, read the extract aloud again, trying to give greater life to your performance.

3 What details in the extract show that it was written at the beginning of the twentieth century?

4 Which of these words best describes the attitude of each man to Eliza Doolittle: sympathetic, fascinated, patronising, rude, arrogant, unfeeling?

Be ready to support your decision with evidence from the text.

Assignments

1 What happens next? Does Higgins agree to give Eliza lessons? Continue the play, keeping the characterisation and style as close as possible to the original.

2 What does Eliza Doolittle think of Professor Higgins? What does he think of her? Write two monologues in which they both discuss their impressions of the other character – what they like and dislike.

3 Does accent matter? Do we judge people according to the way we speak? Do people who use southern English accents gain more respect than people from industrial or very rural areas (compare London accents with Birmingham or Somerset)?

Write a personal essay in which you discuss one of the following:

- your own accent and the language background of your family
- accents which you like and dislike, trying as precisely as possible to explain your preferences
- whether accent should matter.

WIDER READING

Language issues

The most readable and entertaining books about the English language are:

Bill Bryson, *Mother Tongue*; David Crystal, *The English Language*; McCrum, Cran and MacNeill, *The Story of English*; Shirley Russell, *Grammar, Meaning and Style*; Betty Rosen, *And None Of It Was Nonsense*.

Love Poetry

There are many anthologies on the market. The following, which contain a variety of poems, not just love poems, are particularly recommended:

Benson, Chernaik and Herbert, *One Hundred Poems on the Underground*; Brian Patten, *Notes to the Hurrying Man*; Emily Dickinson, *Selected Poems*; Fleur Adcock, *The Faber Book of Twentieth-Century Women's Poetry*.

AFTER READING

1 Based on your reading of language issues, write a personal account of the way in which you learnt to talk, read and write, relating your own memories to some of the theories you will have read about.

2 Choose two poets from different ages and compare some of their love poems in detail. Does the experience of love ultimately seem the same across the centuries?

LAW AND ORDER

Many people believe that standards of behaviour and morality have changed since their day, and not for the better. Older people seem to be constantly concerned about the behaviour of today's teenagers, but was morality and justice really better in the past?
- *Are you, as a young person, honest, courteous and well behaved?*
- *Have standards of behaviour declined or improved over the past 100 years?*

THE YOUTH OF TODAY

■ What are teenagers' attitudes towards the law? The two newspaper articles which follow examine the morality of today's youth.

READING SKILLS
Seeking information
Developing personal response

TEENAGERS MORE TOLERANT OF CRIME

By Richard Spencer

Young people are half as likely again to be let off crime with a caution as their predecessors, a survey of attitudes to youth crime concludes today.

Seventy-four per cent of 13 to 17 year olds who had been in trouble for a criminal offence said they were let off with a caution. Of adults, only half said they were cautioned at the same age.

The survey, by Gallup for the insurance company General Accident, adds credence to the belief that young people getting away with a warning is one of the causes of crime, along with others such as lack of money and boredom.

It also suggests that fewer young people than adults have a strict definition of right and wrong. While teenagers and adults mostly agree on what behaviour is unacceptable, a larger minority of 13 to 17 year olds is tolerant of a variety of crimes.

The young are also more likely to have committed crimes, by their own admission, and more likely to know others who have. The vast majority of teenagers and adults found crimes such as "joy-riding", stealing cars to sell and drug-pushing "unacceptable". But while most also gave the same response for burglary, shoplifting, and under-age driving, some teenagers were equivocal.

Twelve per cent said burglary was just "not very acceptable", compared to six per cent of adults; 37 per cent said the same of shoplifting from a supermarket (22 per cent) and

39 per cent said it of under-age driving (21 per cent).

One in 10 teenagers questioned said shoplifting was acceptable, and nine per cent said the same of under-age driving. Large numbers of teenagers found under-age drinking (56 per cent), under-age sex at 15 (41 per cent) and carrying a weapon for self-protection (39 per cent) acceptable.

Most people attributed youth crime to lack of money and the "buzz factor".

The Government-backed crime prevention charity Crime Concern, which has conducted its own surveys with young people, said the findings mirrored its own.

Mr Nigel Whiskin, chief executive, said it showed much crime was preventable, but that communities should tackle the boredom that was the other side of the coin to the "buzz factor".

Gallup interviewed 980 teenagers, aged 13 to 17, and 428 adults.

The two most common reasons given for the increase in youth crime by both age groups were greater selfishness in society and less parental discipline.

The survey was intended to focus on youth crime, but it does not give adults cause for complacency. Fewer than a third of all over-18s claimed to be "completely honest in all matters", and 34 per cent admitted to misdemeanours such as paying workmen "cash-in-hand", fiddling expenses or bouncing a cheque within the last year.

THE DAILY TELEGRAPH

AFTER READING

1 Look again at the findings of the survey. Did you find any of these statistics surprising, or did you feel that you knew much of this already?

■ In the following article, the writer suggests a reason for the decline of morality among the young.

A Wrong Turn in Teaching Morality

In a society where differences between right and wrong are increasingly blurred, how are children to differentiate between them? Former Anglican priest and author Peter Mullen gives his view.

IN MICHELANGELO'S masterpiece *The Last Judgement* in the Sistine Chapel, Adam is pictured descending into Hell. All the terrors of that fearful place lie before him. But Adam covers only one of his eyes: the other remains open, staring in horrified fascination at the lurid scenes in the inferno....

We need to recognise evil for what it is; but in order

to recognise it we need to be taught. The difference between good and evil has to be learned like any other branch of knowledge. The Prayer Book and old-fashioned religious upbringing always recognised this fact and children were made to learn by heart the Catechism, the precise details of their duty to God and their neighbour.

This is no longer done. The modern age hates the idea of things learned by heart and it dismisses that warm-hearted heartfelt practice by mechanising it in the nasty phrase "by rote". Similarly, the concept of duty has disappeared to be replaced by the universal consumer language of "rights".

No one in high educational places seems to have grasped the fact that rights imply duties and you can't have one without the other.

Old-fashioned RE in schools was never perfect. Anyone who would "volunteer" got the job of teaching it. But at least there was some attempt to teach the difference between right and wrong and, more importantly, it was actually believed that there was a difference and that the difference could be spelled out.

In other words, certain religious and moral statements were generally regarded as true; therefore we were taught the Creed, the Lord's Prayer and the Ten Commandments. Modern RE teaching, where it exists at all, has replaced the Ten Commandments with the Ten Suggestions. There is a reluctance among educationalists to appear "judgmental". Moral absolutes are rejected in favour of moral opinions.

No religion is taught as if it were true. A pluralistic society has placed agreed RE syllabuses in all our schools which offer children a quick trip around the supermarket of faiths: "Hindus believe this and Christians believe that. Jews believe the other and Muslims believe something else. What do you believe, Sharon?"

How is Sharon, aged 12, expected to decide? On the basis of what is she expected to arbitrate among the grand abstractions and develop a sound religious belief?

The truth is, of course, that she is not expected to develop a religious belief at all but to acquire a sophisticated and dispassionate attitude to all religions and none. This is liberal, modern education in practice and it may be encapsulated in a single slogan: Absolute Relativism Rules OK.

It is not OK. It is a crime against our children and a dereliction of our duty to deprive them of a religious and moral upbringing. It is a travesty of religion and morality. For what use is a religion that is only partly, provisionally or perhaps true? What use is morality that has been reduced to a mere matter of opinion?

THE YORKSHIRE POST

AFTER READING

1 What is the main point the writer makes?

2 "It is a crime against our children to deprive them of a religious and moral upbringing." What does this statement mean? Do you agree or disagree with it?

COMPARE

Discussion

1 What evidence do both newspaper reports present to support their case that young people's attitudes have changed from previous generations'? Discuss this in pairs.

2 How do the two articles differ? Which is more factual, and which contains more opinion? Give examples to support your views.

3 Do the attitudes in the articles reflect the views of people in your class? Carry out a survey and compare the results.

4 What arguments would you use to present the opposite point of view – that young people, in many ways, behave better than older people?

5 What are the ten most important laws, in your opinion? What is the most important of the ten?

Assignments

1 Under the heading <u>Problems</u> list the reasons that are put forward in the article 'Teenagers More Tolerant of Crime' for the crime amongst young people.

Under the heading <u>Solutions</u> list the suggestions that the author of 'A Wrong Turn in Teaching Morality' makes to improve the behaviour and attitudes of young people.

Look carefully at both lists and answer the following questions:

i) Do any of the points in the 'Solutions' list answer the points in the problems list?
ii) What suggestions would you make to answer the points in your 'Problems' list that remain unanswered by the points in the 'Solutions' list?

2 Write a speech answering the following question: What do young people need in order to live a good life? The following questions might help you to plan your speech:

- Are young people today better or worse (or similarly) behaved than previous generations?
- What problems do young people have living in today's society? Are these problems responsible in any way for young people's behaviour and attitudes?
- What would you like to see happening to improve the life chances of young people today?

When you have finished, give your speech to other people in your class.

3 Research your rights up to the age of twenty-one, then complete this list:

At birth	Have an account in your name at a bank or building society, and hold Premium Bonds
At 5 years	Must go to school
At 7 years	Can draw money from Post Office Go to a 'U' film with an adult
At 10 years	Can be convicted of a criminal offence

When you have finished, decide what, if anything, you would change and why.

THE COURT OF JUSTICE ═══════

■ Courts have existed since ancient times. They are meant to be places where people can go to obtain justice. However, the rights and wrongs of a case are not always easy to judge, as the following three extracts show.

Set in the 1930s in Alabama, USA, this book contains one of the most famous trial scenes of all time. An African American, Tom Robinson, has been accused of raping a white girl, Mayella Ewell. At this point in the story Atticus Finch, the lawyer defending Tom Robinson, is cross-examining Mayella.

READING SKILLS
Identifying key points
Summarising

To Kill A Mockingbird

Atticus got up grinning, but instead of walking to the witness stand, he opened his coat and hooked his thumbs in his vest, then he walked slowly across the room to the windows. He looked out, but didn't seem especially interested in what he saw, then he turned and strolled back to the witness stand. From long years of experience, I could tell he was trying to come to a decision about something.

'Miss Mayella,' he said, smiling, 'I won't try to scare you for a while, not yet. Let's just get acquainted. How old are you?'

'Said I was nineteen, said it to the judge yonder.' Mayella jerked her head resentfully at the bench.

'So you did, so you did, ma'am. You'll have to bear with me, Miss Mayella, I'm getting along and can't remember as well as I used to. I might ask you things you've already said before, but you'll give me answer, won't you? Good.'

I could see nothing in Mayella's expression to justify Atticus's assumption that he had secured her wholehearted cooperation. She was looking at him furiously.

'Won't answer a word you say long as you keep on mockin' me,' she said.

'Ma'am?' asked Atticus, startled.

'Long's you keep on makin' fun o' me.'

Judge Taylor said, 'Mr Finch is not making fun of you. What's the matter with you?'

Mayella looked from under lowered eyelids at Atticus, but she said to the judge: 'Long's he keeps on callin' me ma'am an' sayin' Miss Mayella. I don't hafta take his sass, I ain't called upon to take it.'

Atticus resumed his stroll to the windows and let Judge Taylor handle this one. Judge Taylor was not the kind of figure that ever evoked pity, but I did feel a pang for him as he tried to explain. 'That's just Mr Finch's way,' he told Mayella. 'We've done business in this court for years and years, and Mr Finch is always courteous to everybody. He's not trying to mock you, he's trying to be polite. That's just his way.'

The judge leaned back. 'Atticus, let's get on with these proceedings, and let the record show that the witness has not been sassed, her views to the contrary.'

I wondered if anybody had ever called her 'ma'am' or

'Miss Mayella' in her life; probably not, as she took offence to routine courtesy. What on earth was her life like? I soon found out.

'You say you're nineteen,' Atticus resumed. 'How many sisters and brothers have you?' He walked from the windows back to the stand.

'Seb'm,' she said, and I wondered if they were all like the specimen I had seen the first day I started to school.

'You the eldest? The oldest?'

'Yes.'

'How long has your mother been dead?'

'Don't know – long time.'

'Did you ever go to school?'

'Read'n'write good as Papa yonder.'

Mayella sounded like a Mr Jingle in a book I had been reading.

'How long did you go to school?'

'Two year – three year – dunno.'

Slowly but surely I began to see the pattern of Atticus's questions: from questions that to Mr Gilmer did not seem sufficiently irrelevant or immaterial to object to, Atticus was quietly building up before the jury a picture of the Ewells' home life. The jury learned the following things: their relief cheque was far from enough to feed the family, and there was strong suspicion that Papa drank it up anyway – he sometimes went off in the swamp for days and came home sick; the weather was seldom cold enough to require shoes, but when it was, you could make dandy ones from strips of old tyres; the family hauled its water in buckets from a spring that ran out at one end of the dump – they kept the surrounding area clear of trash – and it was everybody for himself as far as keeping clean went: if you wanted to wash you hauled your own water; the younger children had perpetual colds and suffered from chronic ground-itch; there was a lady who came around sometimes and asked Mayella why she didn't stay in school – she wrote down the answer; with two members of the family reading and writing, there was no need for the rest of them to learn – Papa needed them at home.

'Miss Mayella,' said Atticus, in spite of himself, 'a nineteen-year-old girl like you must have friends. Who are your friends?' The witness frowned as if puzzled. 'Friends?'

'Yes, don't you know anyone near your age, or older, or younger? Boys and girls? Just ordinary friends?'

Mayella's hostility, which had subsided to grudging neutrality, flared again. 'You makin' fun o' me agin, Mr Finch?' Atticus let her question answer his.

'Do you love your father, Miss Mayella?' was his next.

'Love him, whatcha mean?'

'I mean, is he good to you, is he easy to get along with?'

'He does tollable, 'cept when –'

'Except when?'

Mayella looked at her father, who was sitting with his chair tipped against the railing. He sat up straight and waited for her to answer.

'Except when nothin',' said Mayella. 'I said he does tollable.'

Mr Ewell leaned back again.

'Except when he's drinking?' asked Atticus so gently that Mayella nodded.

'Does he ever go after you?'

'How you mean?'

'When he's – riled, has he ever beaten you?'

Mayella looked around, down at the court reporter, up at the judge. 'Answer the question, Miss Mayella,' said Judge Taylor.

'My paw's never touched a hair o' my head in my life,' she declared firmly. 'He never touched me.'

HARPER LEE

AFTER READING

1 What impression do we get of Mayella Ewell's life from her answers to Atticus's questions?

2 Do you think Mayella makes a reliable witness? Give reasons for your view.

3 What are your impressions of Atticus Finch?

■ Set in Ethiopia, this traditional folk tale shows that, even where great mistakes are made, all can end well.

JUSTICE

A WOMAN one day went out to look for her goats that had wandered away from the herd. She walked back and forth over the fields for a long time without finding them. She came at last to a place by the side of the road where a deaf man sat before a fire brewing himself a cup of coffee. Not realising he was deaf, the woman asked:

'Have you seen my herd of goats come this way?'

The deaf man thought she was asking for the water-hole, so he pointed vaguely toward the river.

The woman thanked him and went to the river. And there, by coincidence, she found the goats. But a young kid had fallen among the rocks and broken its foot.

She picked it up to carry it home. As she passed the place where the deaf man sat drinking his coffee, she stopped to thank him for his help. And in gratitude she offered him the kid.

But the deaf man didn't understand a word she was saying.

When she held the kid toward him he thought she was accusing him of the animal's misfortune, and he became very angry.

'I had nothing to do with it!' he shouted.

'But you pointed the way,' the woman said.

'It happens all the time with goats!' the man shouted.

'I found them right where you said they would be,' the woman replied.

'Go away and leave me alone, I never saw him before in my life!' the man shouted.

People who came along the road stopped to hear the argument. The woman explained to them:

'I was looking for the goats and he pointed toward the river. Now I wish to give him this kid.'

'Do not insult me in this way!' the man shouted loudly. 'I am not a legbreaker!' And in his anger he struck the woman with his hand!'

'Ah, did you see? He struck me with his hand!' the woman said to the people. 'I will take him before the judge!'

So the woman with the kid in her arms, the deaf man, and the spectators went to the house of the judge. The judge came out before his house to listen to the complaint. First, the woman talked, then the man talked, then people in the crowd talked. The judge sat nodding his head. But that meant very little, for the judge, like the man before him, was very deaf. Moreover he was also very near-sighted.

At last, he put up his hand and the talking stopped. He gave them his judgement.

'Such family rows are a disgrace to the Emperor and an affront to the Church,' he said solemnly. He turned to the man.

'From this time forward, stop mistreating your wife,' he said.

He turned to the woman with the young goat in her arms. 'As for you, do not be so lazy. Hereafter do not be late with your husband's meals.'

He looked at the baby goat tenderly.

'And as for the beautiful infant, may she have a long life and grow to be a joy to you both!'

The crowd broke up and the people went their various ways. 'Ah, how good it is!' they said to each other. 'How did we ever get along before justice was given to us?'

TRADITIONAL

AFTER READING

1 What are the misunderstandings that occur between the different characters in the story?

2 Has 'justice' been done?

The Lord of the Flies

A group of young boys have been stranded on a tropical island during a war. This scene comes from a crucial part in the book in which Ralph, who has been elected chief, is attempting to reassert his authority as law and order are beginning to break down. This takes place in an assembly, a children's court, in which the rules of their society are discussed and formed.

The boy holding the conch – a large shell, as shown in the illustration – is allowed to speak.

'The thing is: we need an assembly.'

No one said anything but the faces turned to Ralph were intent. He flourished the conch. He had learnt as a practical business that fundamental statements like this had to be said at least twice, before everyone understood them. One had to sit, attracting all eyes to the conch, and drop words like heavy round stones among the little groups that crouched or squatted. He was searching his mind for simple words so that even the littluns would understand what the assembly was about. Later perhaps, practised debaters – Jack, Maurice, Piggy – would use their whole art to twist the meeting: but now at the beginning the subject of the debate must be laid out clearly.

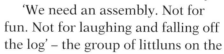

'We need an assembly. Not for fun. Not for laughing and falling off the log' – the group of littluns on the twister giggled and looked at each other – 'not for making jokes, or for' – he lifted the conch in an effort to find the compelling word – 'for cleverness. Not for these things. But to put things straight.'

He paused for a moment.

'I've been along. By myself I went, thinking what's what. I know what we need. An assembly to put things straight. And first of all, I'm speaking.'

He paused for a moment and automatically pushed back his hair. Piggy tiptoed to the triangle, his ineffectual protest made, and joined the others.

Ralph went on.

'We have lots of assemblies. Everybody enjoys speaking and being together. We decide things. But they don't get done. We were going to have water brought from the stream and left in those coco-nut shells under fresh leaves. So it was, for a few days. Now there's no water. The shells are dry. People drink from the river.'

There was a murmur of assent.

'Not that there's anything wrong with drinking from the river. I mean I'd sooner have water from that place – you know – the pool where the waterfall is – than out of an old coco-nut shell. Only we said we'd have the water brought. And now not. There were only two full shells there this afternoon.'

He licked his lips.

'Then there's huts. Shelters.'

The murmur swelled again and died away.

'You mostly sleep in shelters. To-night, except for Samneric [the twins, Sam and Eric] up by the fire, you'll all sleep there. Who built the shelters?'

Clamour rose at once. Everyone had built the shelters. Ralph had to wave the conch once more.

'Wait a minute! I mean, who built all three? We all built the first one, four of us the second, and me 'n Simon built the last one over there. That's why it's so tottery. No. Don't laugh. That shelter might fall down if the rain comes back. We'll need those shelters then.'

He paused and cleared his throat.

'There's another thing. We chose those rocks right along beyond the bathing-pool as a lavatory. That was sensible too. The tide cleans the place up. You littluns know about that.'

There were sniggers here and there and swift glances.

'Now people seem to use anywhere. Even near the shelters and the platform. You littluns, when you're getting fruit; if you're taken short – '

The assembly roared.

'I said if you're taken short you keep away from the fruit. That's dirty.'

Laughter rose again.

'I said that's dirty!'

He plucked at his stiff, grey shirt.

'That's really dirty. If you're taken short you go right along the beach to the rocks. See?'

Piggy held out his hands for the conch but Ralph shook his head. This speech was planned, point by point.

'We've all got to use the rocks again. This place is getting dirty.' He paused. The assembly, sensing a crisis, was tensely expectant. 'And then: about the fire.'

Ralph let out his spare breath with a little gasp that was echoed by his audience. Jack started to chip a piece of wood with this knife and whispered something to Robert, who looked away.

'The fire is the most important thing on the island. How can we ever be rescued except by luck, if we don't keep a fire going? Is a fire too much for us to make?'

He flung out an arm.

'Look at us! How many are we? And yet we can't keep a fire going to make smoke. Don't you understand? Can't you see we ought to – ought to die before we let the fire out?'

There was a self-conscious giggling among the hunters. Ralph turned on them passionately.

'You hunters! You can laugh! But I tell you the smoke is more important than the pig, however often you kill one. Do all of you see?' He spread his arms wide and turned to the whole triangle.

'We've got to make smoke up there – or die'

He paused, feeling for his next point.

'And another thing.'

Someone called out.

'Too many things.'

There came mutters of agreement. Ralph overrode them.

'And another thing. We nearly set the whole island on fire. And we waste time, rolling rocks, and making little cooking fires. Now I say this and make it a rule, because I'm chief. We won't have a fire anywhere but on the mountain. Ever.'

There was a row immediately. Boys stood up and shouted and Ralph shouted back.

'Because if you want a fire to cook fish or crab, you can jolly well go up the mountain. That way we'll be certain.'

Hands were reaching for the conch in the light of the setting sun. He held on and leapt on the trunk.

'All this I meant to say. Now I've said it. You voted me for chief. Now you do what I say'

They quietened, slowly, and at last were seated again. Ralph dropped down and spoke in his ordinary voice.

'So remember. The rocks for a lavatory. Keep the fire going and smoke showing as a signal. Don't take fire from the mountain. Take your food up there.'

Jack stood up, scowling in the gloom, and held out his hands.

'I haven't finished yet.'

'But you've talked and talked!'

'I've got the conch.'

Jack sat down, grumbling.

'Then the last thing. This is what people can talk about.'

He waited till the platform was very still.

'Things are breaking up. I don't understand why. We began well; we were happy. And then –'

He moved the conch gently, looking beyond them at nothing, remembering the beastie, the snake, the fire, the talk of fear.

'Then people started getting frightened.'

A murmur, almost a moan, rose and passed away. Jack had stopped whittling. Ralph went on, abruptly.

'But that's littluns' talk. We'll get that straight. So the last part, the bit we can all talk about, is kind of deciding on the fear.'

The hair was creeping into his eyes again.

'We've got to talk about this fear and decide there's nothing in it. I'm frightened myself, sometimes; only that's nonsense! Like bogies. Then, when we've decided, we can start again and be careful about things like the fire.' A picture of three boys walking along the bright beach flitted through his mind. 'And be happy.'

Ceremonially, Ralph laid the conch on the trunk beside him as a sign that the speech was over. What sunlight reached them was level.

WILLIAM GOLDING

AFTER READING

1 What evidence is there that law and order on the island are breaking down?

2 Find three examples of Ralph's use of 'simple words' so that the 'littluns' would understand.

COMPARE

Discussion

1 What are the differences between each of the three cases?

2 Choose two words from each of the passages that best describe the idea of justice. Then say why you think each of these words is appropriate.

3 Discuss what you think might be the outcome of each of the three cases. Back up your views with reference to each extract.

Assignments

1 What similarities and what differences are there between the characters of Atticus and Ralph? Give reasons for your view, and back these up with evidence from both passages.

2 Imagine that you are a court reporter. Write an account of the case that you found most interesting. Remember to include the following points in your account:

- the setting
- the main characters involved in the case
- the case or the issue that is being judged or decided
- relevant quotations from the main characters in the case.

3 Continue the story of *The Lord of the Flies*. How do the other boys respond to Ralph's speech?

CRIME AND PUNISHMENT

■ Society demands that people are punished for their wrongdoings. However, ideas of what fair punishment is have changed over the centuries, as the following three passages demonstrate.

As the first convicts arrive in the new territory of Australia, the administrators and governors of the colony discuss suitable punishments for the crimes that the convicts have committed on board ship as they travelled half way across the world.

READING SKILLS

Developing personal response

Reading aloud

Our Country's Good

Sydney Cove: GOVERNOR ARTHUR PHILLIP, JUDGE DAVID COLLINS, CAPTAIN WATKIN TENCH, MIDSHIPMAN HARRY BREWER.

The men are shooting birds.

PHILLIP: Was it necessary to cross fifteen thousand miles of ocean to erect another Tyburn?

TENCH: I should think it would make the convicts feel at home.

COLLINS: This land is under English law. The court found them guilty and sentenced them accordingly. There: a baldeyed corella.

PHILLIP: But hanging?

COLLINS: Only the three who were found guilty of stealing from the colony's stores. And that, over there on the Eucalyptus, is a flock of 'cacatua galerita' – the sulphur-crested cockatoo. You have been made Governor-in-Chief of a paradise of birds, Arthur.

PHILLIP: And I hope not of a human hell, Davey. Don't shoot yet, Watkin, let's observe them. Could we not be more humane?

TENCH: Justice and humaneness have never gone hand in hand. The law is not a sentimental comedy.

PHILLIP: I am not suggesting they go without punishment. It is the spectacle of hanging I object to. The convicts will feel nothing has changed and will go back to their old ways.

TENCH: The convicts never left their old ways, Governor, nor do they intend to.

PHILLIP: Three months is not long enough to decide that. You're speaking too loud, Watkin.

COLLINS: I commend your endeavour to oppose the baneful influence of vice with the harmonising acts of civilisation, Governor, but I suspect your edifice

will collapse without the mortar of fear.

PHILLIP: Have these men lost all fear of being flogged?

COLLINS: John Arscott has already been sentenced to 150 lashes for assault.

TENCH: The shoulder blades are exposed at about 100 lashes and I would say that somewhere between 250 and 500 lashes you are probably condemning a man to death anyway.

COLLINS: With the disadvantage that the death is slow, unobserved and cannot serve as a sharp example.

PHILLIP: Harry?

HARRY: The convicts laugh at hangings, sir. They watch them all the time.

TENCH: It's their favourite form of entertainment, I should say.

PHILLIP: Perhaps because they've never been offered anything else.

TENCH: Perhaps we should build an opera house for the convicts.

PHILLIP: We learned to love such things because they were offered to us when we were children or young men. Surely no one is born naturally cultured? I'll have the gun now.

COLLINS: We don't even have any books here, apart from the odd play and a few Bibles. And most of the convicts can't read, so let us return to the matter in hand, which is the punishment of the convicts, not their education.

PHILLIP: Who are the condemned men, Harry?

HARRY: Thomas Barrett, age 17. Transported seven years for stealing one ewe sheep.

PHILLIP: Seventeen!

TENCH: It does seem to prove that the criminal tendency is innate.

PHILLIP: It proves nothing.

HARRY: James Freeman, age 25, Irish, transported 14 years for assault on a sailor at Shadwell Dock.

COLLINS: I'm surprised he wasn't hanged in England.

HARRY: Handy Baker, marine and the thieves' ringleader.

COLLINS: He pleaded that it was wrong to put the convicts

and the marines on the same rations and that he could not work on so little food. He almost swayed us.

TENCH: I do think that was an unfortunate decision, Governor. My men are in a ferment of discontent.

COLLINS: Our Governor-in-Chief would say it is justice, Tench, and so it is. It is also justice to hang these men.

TENCH: The sooner the better, I believe. There is much excitement in the colony about the hangings. It's their theatre, Governor, you cannot change that.

PHILLIP: I would prefer them to see real plays: fine language, sentiment.

TENCH: No doubt Garrick would relish the prospect of eight months at sea for the pleasure of entertaining a group of criminals and the odd savage.

PHILLIP: I never liked Garrick, I always preferred Macklin.

COLLINS: I'm a Kemble man myself. We will need a hangman.

PHILLIP: Harry, you will have to organise the hangings and eventually find someone who agrees to fill that hideous office.

PHILLIP shoots

COLLINS: Shot.

TENCH: Shot.

HARRY: Shot, sir.

COLLINS: It is my belief the hangings should take place tomorrow. The quick execution of justice for the good of the colony, Governor.

PHILLIP: The good of the colony? Oh, look! We've frightened a kangaroo.

HARRY: There is also Dorothy Handland, 82, who stole a biscuit from Robert Sideway.

PHILLIP: Surely we don't have to hang an 82-year-old woman?

COLLINS: That will be unnecessary. She hanged herself this morning.

TIMBERLAKE WERTENBAKER

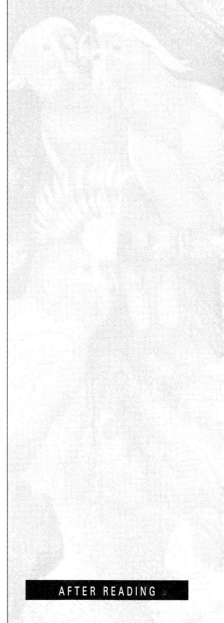

AFTER READING

1 What crimes have the prisoners on the ship been convicted for, and what is their punishment?

2 What differences of opinion are there between the officers about the way to treat the convicts?

■ This traditional American ballad tells the story of a girl who is betrayed by her lover.

Frankie and Johnny

Frankie and Johnny were lovers.
O my Gawd how they did love!
They swore to be true to each other,
As true as the stars above.
He was her man but he done her wrong.

Frankie went down to the hock-shop,
Went for a bucket of beer,
Said: 'O Mr Bartender
Has my loving Johnny been here?
He is my man but he's doing me wrong.'

'I don't want to make you no trouble,
I don't want to tell you no lie,
But I saw Johnny an hour ago
With a girl named Nelly Bly,
He is your man but he's doing you wrong.'

Frankie went down to the hotel,
She didn't go there for fun,
'Cause underneath her kimona
She toted a 44 Gun.
He was her man but he done her wrong.

Frankie went down to the hotel.
She rang the front-door bell,
Said:'Stand back all you chippies
Or I'll blow you all to hell.
I want my man for he's doing me wrong.'

Frankie looked in through the key-hole
And there before her eye
She saw her Johnny on the sofa
A-loving up Nelly Bly.
He was her man; he was doing her wrong

Frankie threw back her kimona,
Took out a big 44,
Root-a-toot-toot, three times she shot
Right through that hardware door.
He was her man but he was doing her wrong.

Johnny grabbed up his Stetson,
Said:'O my Gawd Frankie don't shoot!'
But Frankie pulled hard on the trigger
And the gun went root-a-toot-toot.
She shot her man who was doing her wrong.

'Roll me over easy,
Roll me over slow,
Roll me over on my right side
'Cause my left side hurts me so.
I was her man but I done her wrong.'

'Bring out your rubber-tired buggy,
Bring out your rubber-tired hack;
I'll take my Johnny to the graveyard
But I won't bring him back.
He was my man but he done me wrong.

'Lock me in that dungeon,
Lock me in that cell,
Lock me where the north-east wind
Blows from the corner of Hell.
I shot my man 'cause he done me wrong.'

It was not murder in the first degree,
It was not murder in the third.
A woman simply shot her man
As a hunter drops a bird.
She shot her man 'cause he done her wrong.

Frankie said to the Sheriff,
'What do you think they'll do?'
The Sheriff said to Frankie,
'It's the electric-chair for you.
You shot your man 'cause he done you wrong.'

Frankie sat in the jail-house,
Had no electric fan,
Told her sweet little sister:
'There ain't no good in a man.
I had a man but he done me wrong.'

Once more I saw Frankie,
She was sitting in the Chair
Waiting for to go and meet her God
With the sweat dripping out of her hair.
He was a man but he done her wrong.

This story has no moral,
This story has no end,
This story only goes to show
That there ain't no good in men.
He was her man but he done her wrong.

TRADITIONAL

AFTER READING

1 Who committed the greater crime, Frankie or Johnny?

2 What sort of woman was Frankie?

3 Do you agree that 'This story has no moral'?

■ Alan K, aged twenty-nine, was sentenced to ten years for using a firearm. He wrote the following poem in jail.

Do you know why you're doing it?

Do you know why you are doing it? You would say
You are doing it sadly out of regrettable necessity
And because you are unable to think of any alternative.
Perhaps in a moment of honesty you would admit too
That you are doing it in retaliation for the harm
And the anger we have caused you and your society.

Do you know what it is you are doing though?
Do you want to know or would you sooner not?
If you don't want to know though this still
Won't alter what you are doing, knowing or unknowing.

If you like to put it so we have demeaned others and
Therefore you are demeaning us. But you cannot
Separate us humans: we are all indivisible and
Some of what you do to us you do to yourself.
You are not cleansing us, purging us, reforming us.
The anger and punishment you pour on us only
Generates retaliatory anger in us towards you
And the desire to get our own back. After all
We are not noble characters as you would be first to agree.
We do not ask for pity, sympathy, even forgiveness,
All we ask is that you think about what you are doing
And if you are satisfied go on but if you are not
Then stop. We cannot get out from the horizon-concealing
Walls you have confined us in. But you are freer
To consider in your situation such things as whether
Perhaps you too are also in a prison but a mental one.
Yes, you put our bodies here for a sentence but our
Minds can and still do occasionally escape and fly free.
Do yours? Or are you serving a life-sentence in the
Terrible state of not even knowing you're doing it?

ALAN K.

AFTER READING

1 What does the poet mean when he asks the question 'Do you know why you're doing it?'

2 How much sympathy do you have for the writer?

COMPARE

Discussion

1 What different attitudes are you, the reader, invited to take towards the criminals in the play, the ballad and the poem?

2 Working in small groups, prepare a presentation of either *Our Country's Good* or of 'Frankie and Johnny'. Perform your version to other people in your class.

Assignments

1 'Justice and humaneness have never gone hand in hand.' Do you agree or disagree with this statement? Use it as a starting point for an essay in which you express your views about the issue of crime and punishment.

2 Look in the newspapers for a story that you find interesting. Write a ballad based on this news story, making the events and the characters in it come alive.

WIDER READING

Books with gripping court scenes
Mildred Taylor, *Let the Circle be Unbroken*; E.M Forster, *A Passage to India*; William Shakespeare, *The Merchant of Venice*; John Mortimer, The *Rumpole of the Bailey* series; Scott Turow, *Presumed Innocent*; Gary Kilworth, *Murderer's Walk*.

AFTER READING

1 From your reading, what are the elements that combine to make a good 'Law and Order' story?

2 Write your own short story with a court scene at its centre. Begin the story at the court hearing, and use flashbacks to fill in the reader about what happened before the trial.

BEGINNINGS

For many new writers, the most difficult part of the writing process is getting started. Faced with a blank piece of paper, they simply sit and stare.
- *How do you start writing? How would you begin a novel?*
- *How would you revise a classic Victorian novel for a modern teenage audience? How would you begin a biography of a famous person?*

HOW TO BEGIN

■ Two writers give advice about how to start. The first passage is from the *Yorkshire Evening Press*, and the second is from a book about short-story writing.

READING SKILLS

Reading for meaning

Identifying key points

How to be a writer: tips from the heart

Being a professional writer is not like becoming a hairdresser, a plumber or a member of any other profession. In those cases, it is possible to attend a course or to earn a suitable qualification before embarking on a chosen career.

Most writers are self-taught so there is nothing to prevent a person of any age becoming a professional writer. But where does a budding writer begin? What qualifications are needed? Do you need a university education? How do you submit work to magazines or publishers? Do you get paid?

The first thing to remember is that the scope is enormous. Just walk into a book shop, or into a newsagent's with its magazines, greetings cards and newspapers – then remember that every word there has to be written by somebody! It could be you.

No special qualifications are needed, but you do need a skill with words. You should be able to spell and to compose a grammatical sentence.

Publishers of books, magazines, newspapers and greeting cards are always on the look-out for writers who can produce reliable work. And so are radio and television producers.

The first thing is to decide what you want to write.

If you wish to write for newspapers, then training as a journalist is advised. Write to your local newspaper about career opportunities.

If you want to write verse for greetings cards, look up the address on a card and write to the company, asking for details of their requirements – and what they are prepared to pay! All writing is work, and you should get paid for it.

Writing short stories, books, radio or television scripts is much harder, however. Many writers struggle for years without having their work accepted. They learn by their mistakes.

The secret is to keep working, keep writing and don't let friends or relations criticise your work – they are not qualified to make judgements. Send the material to a publisher, a magazine, or a radio or television producer to get a professional opinion.

Work submitted for publication must be typed in double spacing on A4 paper and, when you send it off, you must enclose a stamped addressed envelope for its return if your article is not suitable.

If you are embarking on a longer work, however, say a non-fiction book about your favourite subject, you should first write to a publisher to outline the idea and to see if an editor is interested. If so, they will provide suitable advice on what to do next.

Fiction books, such as novels, romances or crime stories, are usually judged on the finished product, but you will have to find out which publishers want that sort of book, and if so, how many words the book should contain. The necessary addresses are inside newspapers, magazines or books themselves, or there is the Writer's and Artist's Yearbook, which contains a host of addresses and some valuable advice. Your library will have a copy.

It is very important, however, that you study the requirements of publishers before submitting your work.

How long should an article be? Try counting the words of an article you have just read – like this one. Should the book be illustrated? If so, where do you get pictures from? Should a short story include drugs or violence? Do all novels have a happy ending? You must discover all these answers and more, by reading lots and lots of material.

Locally, there may be creative writing courses or a writers' club – these will make you most welcome and are the ideal starting point for any would-be writer.

You have probably taken your first step to seeing your name in print by reading this article. Good luck – and remember that the harder you work, the luckier you will be.

PETER WALKER

AFTER READING

1 What would you say was the single most important piece of advice Peter Walker gives?

2 What do you think he could have explained in greater detail?

3 Do you agree with his point that friends and relations are not qualified to criticise your work?

Starting a Story

'Where shall I begin my story?' That is the question of every writer of fiction, be he a novice or a household name. For the beginning of a story is the most important part of all. Every story also has a middle and an end which also carry their own measure of importance for the overall effect which the author is trying to achieve. But the beginning bears the main load. Not only does it have to hold the reader's interest, but it has to create that interest in the first place.

Each author tends to develop his own technique in story beginnings. One will start with 'a day that is different'. Another will choose 'a moment of change'. And yet another decides on 'a decision must be made'. All of these are quite valid and, if well written, will appeal to the reader's inherent curiosity.

But the better kind of beginning is the one which seems to be the most reasonable one for that story. Now this may seem to be oversimplifying the problem and hardly answers the question of 'where shall I begin my story?'.

More often than not, we do not truly know our story to its fullest degree until we have written it. So how can we write a beginning that is best suited to it until we know what the story is? The answer is really quite simple. You

1 What is Roy Lomax's single most important piece of advice about starting a story?

2 How important does he say the beginning of a story is?

don't write the beginning until you have written the story in full.

What you do is to write any kind of a beginning which will get you off to a start. It doesn't even have to be a good beginning, because you will eventually come back to it and either scrap or rewrite it. It is as simple as that!

ROY LOMAX
Writing the Short Story

COMPARE

Discussion

1 Which passage makes writing sound easier, which more enjoyable?

2 Which advice do you find most helpful? Say why.

3 In pairs, look at the two writers' styles, and note down the similarities and differences between them.

Assignments

1 Use the following headings to make a list of the ways in which the two passages differ:
- advice
- tone (the kind of language used – is it formal/informal; personal/impersonal?)
- readership (is it general or specialist?)

Give an example for each point you make.

2 Try writing the opening of a short story based in the room you are currently sitting in. Aim to write a piece which:
- catches the reader's attention
- sets the scene/gives a sense of character
- makes the reader want to keep reading.

OR

Choose a certain subject, then write the opening paragraph or verse of the following. The content of each should be the same:
- a newspaper article
- a short story
- a poem.

Then write a paragraph explaining what you tried to achieve and how well it worked.

JANE EYRE

■ Charlotte Brontë's novel *Jane Eyre*, 1847, opens with the orphaned Jane being cruelly treated by her adopted family. Read the original beginning to the novel, and then look at the way two writers have simplified the language of the story for younger readership.

READING SKILLS
Summarising
Developing personal response

Chapter 1

THERE was no possibility of taking a walk that day. We had been wandering, indeed, in the leafless shrubbery an hour in the morning; but since dinner (Mrs Reed, when there was no company, dined early) the cold winter wind had brought with it clouds so sombre, and a rain so penetrating, that further outdoor exercise was now out of the question.

I was glad of it: I never liked long walks, especially on chilly afternoons: dreadful to me was the coming home in the raw twilight, with nipped fingers and toes, and a heart saddened by the chidings of Bessie, the nurse, and humbled by the consciousness of my physical inferiority to Eliza, John, and Georgiana Reed.

The said Eliza, John, and Georgiana were now clustered round their mama in the drawing-room: she lay reclined on a sofa by the fireside, and with her darlings about her (for the time neither quarrelling nor crying) looked perfectly happy. Me, she had dispensed from joining the group; saying, 'She regretted to be under the necessity of keeping me at a distance; but that until she heard from Bessie, and could discover by her own observation, that I was endeavouring in good earnest to acquire a more sociable and childlike disposition, a more attractive and sprightly manner – something lighter, franker, more natural, as it were – she really must exclude me from privileges, intended only for contented, happy, little children.'

'What does Bessie say I have done?' I asked.

'Jane, I don't like cavillers or questioners; besides, there is something truly forbidding in a child taking up her elders in that manner. Be seated somewhere; and until you can speak pleasantly, remain silent.'

A small breakfast-room adjoined the drawing-room, I slipped in there. It contained a bookcase: I soon possessed myself of a volume, taking care that it should be one stored with pictures. I mounted into the window-seat: gathering up my feet, I sat cross-legged, like a Turk; and, having drawn the red moreen curtain nearly close, I was shrined in double retirement.

Folds of scarlet drapery shut in my view to the right

hand; to the left were the clear panes of glass, protecting, but not separating me from the drear November day. At intervals, while turning over the leaves of my book, I studied the aspect of that winter afternoon. Afar, it offered a pale blank of mist and cloud; near a scene of wet lawn and storm-beat shrub, with ceaseless rain sweeping away wildly before a long and lamenting blast.

I returned to my book – Bewick's *History of British Birds*: the letterpress thereof I cared little for, generally speaking; and yet there were certain introductory pages that, child as I was, I could not pass quite as a blank. They were those which treat of the haunts of sea-fowl; of 'the solitary rocks and promontories' by them only inhabited; of the coast of Norway, studded with isles from its southern extremity, the Lindeness, or Naze, to the North Cape:

'Where the Northern Ocean, in vast whirls,
Boils round the naked, melancholy isles
Of farthest Thule; and the Atlantic surge
Pours in among the stormy Hebrides.'

Nor could I pass unnoticed the suggestion of the bleak shores of Lapland, Siberia, Nova Zembla, Iceland, Greenland, with 'the vast sweep of the Arctic Zone, and those forlorn regions of dreary space – that reservoir of frost and snow, where firm fields of ice, the accumulation of centuries of winters, glazed in alpine heights, surround the pole and concentre the multiplied rigours of extreme cold.' Of these death-white realms I formed an idea of my own: shadowy, like all the half-comprehended notions that float dim through children's brains, but strangely impressive. The words in these introductory pages connected themselves with the succeeding vignettes, and gave significance to the rock standing up alone in a sea of billow and spray; to the broken boat stranded on a desolate coast; to the cold and ghastly moon glancing through bars of clout at a wreck just sinking.

I cannot tell what sentiment haunted the quite solitary churchyard, with its inscribed headstone; its gate, its two trees, its low horizon, girdled by a broken wall, and its newly-risen crescent, attesting the hour of eventide.

The two ships becalmed on a torpid sea, I believed to be marine phantoms.

The fiend pinning down the thief's pack behind him, I passed over quickly: it was an object of terror.

So was the black horned thing seated aloof on a rock, surveying a distant crowd surrounding a gallows.

Each picture told a story; mysterious often to my undeveloped understanding and imperfect feelings, yet ever profoundly interesting: as interesting as the tales Bessie sometimes narrated on winter evenings, when she chanced to be in good humour; and when, having brought her ironing-table to the nursery hearth, she allowed us to sit about it, and while she got up Mrs Reed's lace frills, and crimped her nightcap borders, fed our eager attention with passages of love and adventure taken from old fairy tales and other ballads; or (as at a later period I discovered) from the pages of *Pamela,* and *Henry, Earl of Moreland.*

With Bewick on my knee, I was then happy: happy at least in my way. I feared nothing but interruption, and that too soon. The breakfast-room door opened.

'Boh! Madam Mope!' cried the voice of John Reed; then he paused: he found the room apparently empty.

'Where the dickens is she!' he continued. 'Lizzy! Georgy! (calling to his sisters) Joan is not here: tell mama she is run out into the rain – bad animal!'

'It is well I drew the curtain,' thought I; and I wished fervently he might not discover my hiding-place: nor would John Reed have found it out himself; he was not quick either of vision or conception; but Eliza just put her head in at the door, and said at once:

'She is in the window-seat, to be sure, Jack.'

And I came out immediately, for I trembled at the idea of being dragged forth by the said Jack.

'What do you want?' I asked, with awkward diffidence.

'Say, "What do you want, Master Reed?" ' was the answer. 'I want you to come here;' and seating himself in an armchair, he intimated by a gesture that I was to approach and stand before him.

John Reed was a schoolboy of fourteen years old: large and stout for his age, with a dingy and unwholesome skin; thick lineaments in a spacious visage, heavy limbs and large extremities. He gorged himself habitually at table, which made him bilious, and gave him a dim and bleared eye and flabby cheeks. He ought now to have been at school; but his mama had taken him home for a month or two, 'on account of his delicate health.' Mr Miles, the master, affirmed that he would do very well if he had fewer cakes and sweetmeats sent him from home; but the mother's heart turned from an opinion so harsh, and inclined rather to the more refined idea that John's sallowness was owing to over-application and, perhaps, to pining after home.

John had not much affection for his mother and sisters, and an antipathy to me. He bullied and punished me; not two or three times in the week nor once or twice in the day, but continually: every nerve I had feared him, and every morsel of flesh in my bones shrank when he came near. There were moments when I was bewildered by the terror he inspired, because I had no appeal whatever against either his menaces or his inflictions; the servants did not like to offend their young master by taking my part against him, and Mrs Reed was blind and deaf on the subject: she never saw him strike or heard him abuse me, though he did both now and then in her very presence, more frequently, however, behind her back.

Habitually obedient to John, I came up to his chair: he spent some three minutes in thrusting out his tongue at me as far as he could without damaging the roots: I knew he would soon strike, and while dreading the blow, I mused on the disgusting and ugly appearance of him who would presently deal it. I wonder if he read that notion in my face; for, all at once, without speaking, he struck suddenly and strongly. I tottered, and on regaining my equilibrium retired back a step or two from his chair.

'That is for your impudence in answering mama awhile since,' said he, 'and for your sneaking way of getting behind curtains, and for the look you had in your eyes two minutes since, you rat!'

Accustomed to John Reed's abuse, I never had an idea of replying to it; my care was how to endure the blow which would certainly follow the insult.

'What were you doing behind the curtain?' he asked.

'I was reading.'

'Show the book.'

I returned to the window and fetched it thence.

'You have no business to take our books; you are a dependant, mama says; you have no money; your father left you none; you ought to beg, and not to live here with gentlemen's children like us, and eat the same meals we do, and wear clothes at our mama's expense. Now I'll teach you to rummage my bookshelves: for they are mine; all the house belongs to me, or will do in a few years. Go and stand by the door, out of the way of the mirror and windows.'

I did so, not at first aware what was his intention; but when I saw him lift and poise the book and stand in act to hurl it, I instinctively started aside with a cry of alarm: not soon enough, however; the volume was flung, it hit me, and I fell, striking my head against the door and cutting it. The cut bled, the pain was sharp: my terror had passed its climax; other feelings succeeded.

'Wicked and cruel boy!' I said. 'You are like a murderer – you are like a slave-driver – you are like the Roman emperors!'

I had read Goldsmith's *History of Rome*, and had formed my opinion of Nero, Caligula, etc. Also I had drawn parallels in silence, which I never thought thus to have declared aloud.

'What! what!' he cried. 'Did she say that to me? Did you hear her, Eliza and Georgiana? Won't I tell mama? but first–'

He ran headlong at me: I felt him grasp my hair and my shoulder: he had closed with a desperate thing. I really saw in him a tyrant, a murderer. I felt a drop or two of blood from my head trickle down my neck, and was sensible of somewhat pungent suffering: these sensations for the time predominated over fear, and I received him in frantic sort. I don't very well know what I did with my hands, but he called me 'Rat! Rat!' and bellowed out aloud. Aid was near him: Eliza and Georgiana had run for Mrs. Reed, who was gone upstairs: she now came upon the scene, followed by Bessie and her maid Abbot.

We were parted: I heard the words –
'Dear! dear! What a fury to fly at Master John!'
'Did ever anybody see such a picture of passion!'
Then Mrs Reed subjoined –
'Take her away to the red-room, and lock her in there.'
Four hands were immediately laid upon me, and I was borne upstairs.

CHARLOTTE BRONTË

AFTER READING

1 Try to summarise the storyline in three sentences.

2 Write down five words used by Charlotte Brontë which you are not familiar with. Then look closely at the words and make guesses about what they mean.

Discussion

1 Look again at the opening sentence. How successful is it in making you want to read on? Rewrite the sentence in three different ways and compare the effect it has.

2 In pairs, look next at the opening two paragraphs again. What are your first impressions of Jane Eyre – her age, appearance and character?

3 Look at the part of the story where Jane reads Bewick's *History of British Birds*. Which of the following statements best describes her response to the book?

a. Jane is fascinated by the descriptions of the wildlife.
b. Jane is fascinated, not by the wildlife, but by the descriptions of the Arctic.
c. Jane reads too much into what she reads, imagining all kinds of terrors.
d. Jane reads to escape from the cruelties of the Reed family.

4 Look at the description of John Reed. With your partner, think of five words which seem best to describe his attitude to Jane.

Assignments

1 The chapter ends with a moment of tension – Jane being taken away to the 'red room'. Does this make you want to read on or not?

EITHER write a review of the opening chapter, saying whether or not you think it is successful, OR continue the story of Jane's imprisonment in the 'red-room': what do you think happens there? What kind of room is it? How does Jane react?

2 What impressions have you formed of Jane Eyre from this first chapter? Write a character study which mentions her personality, her behaviour and her attitude towards the Reeds. Is your analysis of her character entirely positive?

3 Choose a reference book, perhaps a book about British birds, and write a short story which begins with someone reading it. Gradually their imagination should take over.

JANE EYRE FOR YOUNGER READERS

■ These two versions of *Jane Eyre* were written for younger readers who might find the complexity and length of Charlotte Brontë's original too difficult.

Analysing language

Chapter 1

The Reed Family

It was winter. The weather was very cold and it was raining, We could not go outside. I was glad; I never liked walks with my cousins, John, Eliza and Georgiana Reed. I was not a strong child. I always got tired before they did and then they laughed at me.

I did not like my cousins or my aunt, their mother. They did not like me, either. They never let me play their games. I was very lonely at Gateshead Hall. But I had to live there because I was an orphan: my mother and father had died when I was a baby.

On that cold winter afternoon my cousins were sitting with their mother in the sitting room. My aunt did not allow me to be with them. I went to sit in the library. Reading was one of my greatest pleasures. The books in the library were not children's books, but I loved them.

Suddenly, the door opened and John Reed walked in. Eliza and Georgiana were following him.

"Where are you?" he shouted. "What are you doing? Come here at once!"

I stood up slowly. I was very frightened because John Reed was a big boy. He was fourteen years old and I was only ten. He was tall and very fat, because he ate too much. He was his mother's favourite. In her eyes he did nothing wrong. Suddenly he hit me so hard that I almost fell.

"What were you doing?" he shouted.

"I was reading," I answered quietly.

"Were you reading one of my mother's books?"

"Yes," I replied, and gave him the book.

"You mustn't read our family's books," he said. "You're an orphan; your mother and father are dead; you have no money; you live with us because you have no other family. But you aren't one of our family and we don't like you." He lifted the book and hit my head with it.

For the first time in my life I showed that I was angry. All the unhappiness and loneliness of my life at Gateshead Hall came out.

"Wicked boy!" I cried.

John Reed was very surprised. "What did you say?" he shouted. "Did you hear that, Eliza and Georgiana? I'm going

AFTER READING

1 What has this writer chosen to leave out of the original version of the story?

2 What other changes do you notice – in characters, settings, details or language?

to the sitting room immediately. I'm going to tell Mother about you." Again he came towards me. He was going to hit me again. But this time I was ready, and I hit him first. I had never fought with him before. I pulled his hair and shouted, "You wicked boy! I hate you!" Mrs Reed and Bessie, one of the servants, appeared and pulled me away from my cousin.

"Take her to the red room and lock the door," my aunt said coldly.

Adapted by SUE ULLSTEIN

— • —

Part 1
A Child at Gateshead

We could not go for a walk that afternoon. There was such a freezing cold wind, and such heavy rain, that we all stayed indoors. I was glad of it. I never liked long walks, especially in winter. I used to hate coming home when it was almost dark, with ice-cold fingers and toes, feeling miserable because Bessie, the nursemaid, was always scolding me. All the time I knew I was different from my other cousins, Eliza, John and Georgiana Reed. They were taller and stronger than me, and they were loved.

These three usually spent their time crying and quarrelling, but today they were sitting quietly around their mother in the sitting room. I wanted to join the family circle, but Mrs Reed, my aunt, refused. Bessie had complained about me.

'No, I'm sorry, Jane. Until I hear from Bessie, or see for myself, that you are really trying to behave better, you cannot be treated as a good, happy child, like *my* children.'

'What does Bessie say I have done?' I asked.

'Jane, it is not polite to question me in that way. If you cannot speak pleasantly, be quiet.'

I crept out of the sitting-room and into the small room next door, where I chose a book full of pictures from the bookcase. I climbed on to the window-seat and drew the curtains, so that I was completely hidden. I sat there for a while. Sometimes I looked out of the window at the grey November afternoon, and saw the rain pouring down on the leafless garden. But most of the time I studied the book and stared, fascinated, at the pictures. Lost in the world of imagination, I forgot my sad, lonely existence for a while, and was happy. I was only afraid that my secret hiding-place might be discovered.

Suddenly the door of the room opened. John Reed rushed in.

'Where are you, rat?' he shouted. He did not see me behind the curtain. 'Eliza! Georgy! Jane isn't here! Tell Mamma she's run out into the rain – what a bad animal she is!'

'How lucky I drew the curtain,' I thought. He would never have found me, because he was not very intelligent. But Eliza guessed at once where I was.

'She's in the window-seat, John,' she called from the sitting-room. So I came out immediately, as I did not want him to pull me out.

'What do you want? I asked him.

'Say, "What do you want, *Master* Reed",' he answered, sitting in an armchair. 'I want you to come here.'

John Reed was fourteen and I was only ten. He was large and rather fat. He usually ate too much at meals, which made him ill. He should have been at boarding school, but his mother, who loved him very much, had brought him home for a month or two, because she thought his health was delicate.

John did not love his mother or his sisters, and he hated me. He bullied and punished me, not two or three times a week, not once or twice a day, but all the time. My whole body trembled when he came near. Sometimes he hit me, sometimes he just threatened me, and I lived in terrible fear of him. I had no idea how to stop him. The servants did not want to offend their young master, and Mrs Reed could see no fault in her dear boy.

So I obeyed John's order and approached his armchair, thinking how very ugly his face was. Perhaps he understood what I was thinking, for he hit me hard on the face.

'That is for your rudeness to Mamma just now,' he said, 'and for your wickedness in hiding, and for looking at me like that, you rat!' I was so used to his bullying that I never thought of hitting him back.

'What were you doing behind that curtain?' he asked.

'I was reading,' I answered.

'Show me the book.' I gave it to him.

'You have no right to take our books,' he continued. 'You have no money and your father left you none. You ought to beg in the streets, not live here in comfort with a gentleman's family. Anyway all these books are mine, and so is the whole house, or will be in a few years' time. I'll teach you not to borrow my books again.' He lifted the heavy book and threw it hard at me.

It hit me and I fell, cutting my head on the door. I was in great pain, and suddenly for the first time in my life, I forgot my fear of John Reed.

'You wicked, cruel boy!' I cried. 'You are a bully! You are as bad as a murderer!'

'What! What!' he cried. 'Did she say that to me? Did you hear, Eliza and Georgiana? I'll tell Mamma, but first...'

He rushed to attack me, but now he was fighting with a desperate girl. I really saw him as a wicked murderer. I felt the blood running down my face, and the pain gave me strength. I fought back as hard as I could. My resistance surprised him, and he shouted for help. His sisters ran for Mrs Reed, who called her maid, Miss Abbott, and Bessie. They pulled us apart and I heard them say, 'What a wicked girl! She attacked Master John!'

Mrs Reed said calmly, 'Take her away to the red room and lock her in there.' And so I was carried upstairs, arms waving and legs kicking.

Adapted by CLARE WEST

AFTER READING

1 What has this writer chosen to leave out of the original version of the story?

2 How has she changed the overall content of the chapter?

COMPARE

Discussion

1   Compare the first three paragraphs of both modern versions of the story. What similarities and differences do you notice in the two writers' approaches? Look at language and storyline.

2   Pick out the three most difficult words from each modern version (either by choosing words you are unfamiliar with or by picking those with the most syllables). Compare them with the unfamiliar words you noted down from Charlotte Brontë's version. What do these words suggest about the intended readership?

3   In pairs, discuss and list what each writer has left out of the original version of the story, e.g. complex vocabulary, certain characters, dialogue, description. Put a tick by those decisions which you agree with and a cross by those which you disagree with. Compare your list with another pair's. Which of the modern versions do you prefer and why?

Assignments

1   Imagine that you have been asked to tell the *Jane Eyre* story to five to seven year olds in a picture book format. How would you present the content of the first chapter of the novel in four or five images? What pictures would you use? What words would you put underneath?

Do a rough design of these pictures with captions, and then write a commentary saying why you chose these images, and how you simplified the language and storyline.

2   Do you agree with the idea that classic works of literature should be rewritten or simplified? Have a look at one of the *Shakespeare Made Simple* texts, or watch the video of one of Leon Garfield's *Animated Tales*. Write about what has been lost and gained by adapting the original text.

3   Choose a classic work of literature and adapt the first chapter or scene for a teenage audience. These titles work well: Shakespeare, *The Tempest*; Dickens, *Dombey and Son*; Jane Austen, *Pride and Prejudice*.

Then write a commentary which examines the following:
- cuts/additions to the storyline
- decisions about vocabulary
- decisions about sentence structure
- what has been gained or lost in the process.

IN THE BEGINNING ===

■ Genesis, the first book of the Bible, tells how God created the world and all its creatures. In Chapters 2 and 3, the story of Adam and Eve is told. Compare the original version with the poem which follows.

ﻪﻪﻪﻪ **GENESIS** ﻪﻪﻪﻪ

Chapter 2

THUS the heavens and the earth were finished, and all the host of them.

2 And on the seventh day God ended his work which he had made; and he rested on the seventh day from all his work which he had made.

3 And God blessed the seventh day, and sanctified it: because in it he had rested from all his work which God created and made.

4 These are the generations of the heavens and of the earth when they were created, in the day that the Lord God made the earth and the heavens.

5 And every plant of the field before it was in the earth, and every herb of the field before it grew: For the Lord God had not caused it to rain upon the earth, and there was not a man to till the ground.

6 But there went up a mist from the earth, and watered the whole face of the ground.

7 And the Lord God formed man of the dust of the ground, and breathed into his nostrils the breath of life; and man became a living soul...

21 And the Lord God caused a deep sleep to fall upon Adam, and he slept: and he took one of his ribs, and closed up the flesh instead thereof;

22 And the rib, which the Lord God had taken from man, made he a woman, and brought her unto the man.

23 And Adam said, This is now bone of my bones, and flesh of my flesh: she shall be called Woman, because she was taken out of Man.

24 Therefore shall a man leave his father and his mother, and shall cleave unto his wife: and they shall be one flesh.

25 And they were both naked, the man and his wife, and were not ashamed.

Chapter 3

NOW the serpent was more subtil than any beast of the field which the Lord God had made. And he said unto the woman, Yea, hath God said. Ye shall not eat of every tree of the garden?

2 And the woman said unto the serpent, We may eat of the fruit of the trees of the garden:

3 But of the fruit of the tree which is in the midst of the garden, God hath said, Ye shall not eat of it, neither shall ye touch it, lest ye die.

4 And the serpent said unto the woman, Ye shall not surely die:

5 For God doth know that in the day ye eat thereof, then your eyes shall be opened, and ye shall be as gods, knowing good and evil.

6 And when the woman saw that the tree was good for food, and that it was pleasant to the eyes, and a tree to be desired to make one wise, she took of the fruit thereof, and did eat, and gave also unto her husband with her; and he did eat.

7   And the eyes of them both were opened, and they knew that they were naked; and they sewed fig leaves together, and made themselves aprons.

8   And they heard the voice of the Lord God walking in the garden in the cool of the day: and Adam and his wife hid themselves from the presence of the Lord God amongst the trees of the garden.

9   And the Lord God called unto Adam, and said unto him, Where art thou?

10 And he said, I heard thy voice in the garden, and I was afraid, because I was naked; and I hid myself.

11 And he said, Who told thee that thou wast naked? Has thou eaten of the tree, whereof I commanded thee that thou shouldest not eat?

12 And the man said, The woman whom thou gavest to be with me, she gave of the tree, and I did eat.

13 And the Lord God said unto the woman, What is this that thou hast done? And the woman said, The serpent beguiled me, and I did eat.

14 And the Lord God said unto the serpent, Because thou hast done this, thou art cursed above all cattle, and above every beast of the field; upon thy belly shalt thou go and dust shalt thou eat all the days of thy life:

15 And I will put enmity between thee and the woman, and between thy seed and her seed; it shall bruise thy head, and thou shalt bruise his heel.

16 Unto the woman he said, I will greatly multiply thy sorrow and thy conception; in sorrow thou shalt bring forth children; and thy desire shall be to thy husband, and he shall rule over thee.

17 And unto Adam he said, Because thou hast harkened unto the voice of thy wife, and hast eaten of the tree, of which I commanded thee saying, Thou shalt not eat of it: cursed is the ground for thy sake; in sorrow shalt thou eat of it all the days of thy life;

18 Thorns also and thistles shall it bring forth to thee; and thou shalt eat the herb of the field;

19 In the sweat of thy face shalt thou eat bread, till thou return unto the ground; for out of it wast thou taken: for dust thou art, and unto dust shalt thou return.

20 And Adam called his wife's name Eve; because she was the mother of all living.

21 Unto Adam also and to his wife did the Lord God make coats of skins, and clothed them.

22 And the Lord God said, Behold, the man is become as one of us, to know good and evil: and now, lest he put forth his hand, and take also of the tree of life, and eat, and live for ever:

23 Therefore the Lord God sent him forth from the garden of Eden, to till the ground from whence he was taken.

24 So he drove out the man; and he placed at the east of the garden of Eden Cherubims, and a flaming sword which turned every way, to keep the way of the tree of life.

THE AUTHORIZED VERSION

AFTER READING

1 Why does God create Eve?

2 How is Eve created?

3 What do Adam and Eve do wrong?

Paradise Illustrated

'Where are you, Adam?'
'I'm behind this tree, Lord.'
'What are you doing there?'
'Nothing, Lord. I'm naked is all.'
'Who told you you were naked?'
'I noticed it, Lord.'
'Naked, shmaked, what does it matter?'
'You can get six months for indecency, Lord.'
'What's six months to you, you're immortal.'
'It might give the animals funny thoughts.'
'My animals don't have funny thoughts.'
'The best people wear suits, Lord.'
'You were the best people, Adam.'
'The weather might change, Lord.'
'Too right. It will.'

D J ENRIGHT

AFTER READING

1 Think of three words to describe the character of God and three to describe Adam in the poem.

COMPARE

Discussion

1 Who is mostly to blame for the crime of eating the apple, Adam, Eve or the Serpent? Place them in rank order of guilt and say what part they played. Compare your opinions with the rest of the class.

2 Discuss in pairs what we learn about Adam's character from the Bible extract. Now compare him with the way he is portrayed in the poem.

3 Which of the following words best describes the TONE of each extract – comic, sombre, mocking, neutral, factual, mythical, disrespectful?
Put them in order and explain your choice.

4 Which words and phrases in each extract best demonstrate how old or recent the writing is?

Assignments

1 Some people find the language of the Authorized Version of the Bible very difficult to follow. Take a couple of verses from the extract, and rewrite them in modern English. Then write an explanation of the main changes you have made and the problems you encountered.

2 Some people might find 'Paradise Illustrated' irreverent or disrespectful. Others might say that it tells the Bible story in a more human way. Write about your response to Enright's updated version of the Bible story.

3 The Authorized Version has been described as the most beautifully written English we have. Read the extract through again, and write your own personal response to the story itself and the way it is told. Focus on words and sentences which you particularly like, explaining why they appeal to you.

BIOGRAPHIES OLD AND NEW

■ In 1874, four years after the death of his friend Charles Dickens, John Forster wrote his biography. Almost 120 years later, writer Peter Ackroyd published another biography. This is how the two biographers begin their accounts of Dickens's life.

The Life of
Charles Dickens
❦

Chapter 1

CHARLES DICKENS, the most popular novelist of the century, and one of the greatest humorists that England has produced, was born at Lanport, in Portsea, on Friday, the seventh of February, 1812.

His father, John Dickens, a clerk in the navy pay-office, was at this time stationed in the Portsmouth Dockyard. He had made acquaintance with the lady, Elizabeth Barrow, who became afterwards his wife, through her elder brother, Thomas Barrow, also engaged on the establishment at Somerset House, and she bore him in all a family of eight children, of whom two died in infancy. The eldest, Fanny (born 1810), was followed by Charles (entered in the baptismal register of Portsea as Charles John Huffham, though on the very rare occasions when he subscribed that name he wrote Huffam); by another son, named Alfred, who died in childhood; by Letitia (born 1816); by another daughter, Harriet, who died also in childhood; by Frederick (born 1820); by Alfred Lamert (born 1822); and by Augustus (born 1827).

Walter Scott tells us, in his fragment of autobiography, speaking of the strange remedies applied to his lameness, that he remembered lying on the floor in the parlour of his grandfather's farmhouse, swathed up in a sheepskin warm from the body of the sheep, being then not three years old. David Copperfield's memory goes beyond this. He represents himself seeing so far back into the blank of his infancy as to discern therein his mother and her servant, dwarfed to his sight by stooping down or kneeling on the floor, and himself going unsteadily from the one to the other. He admits this may be fancy, though he believes the power of observation in numbers of very young children to be quite wonderful for its closeness and accuracy, and thinks that the recollection of most of us can go farther back into such times than many of us suppose. But what he adds is certainly not fancy. "If it should appear from anything I may set down in this narrative that I was a child of close observation, or that as a man I have a strong memory of my childhood, I undoubtedly lay claim to both of these characteristics." Applicable as it might be to David Copperfield, this was unaffectedly true of Charles Dickens.

He has often told me that he remembered the small front garden to the house at Portsea, from which he was taken away when he was two years old, and where, watched by a nurse through a low kitchen window almost level with the gravel walk, he trotted about with something to eat, and his little elder sister with him. He was carried from the garden one day to see the soldiers exercise; and I perfectly recollect that, on our being at Portsmouth together while he was writing *Nickleby*, he recognised the exact shape of the military parade seen by him as a very infant, on the same spot, a quarter of a century before.

When his father was again brought up by his duties to London from Portsmouth, they went into lodgings in Norfolk Street, Middlesex Hospital; and it lived also in the child's memory that they had come away from Portsea in the snow. Their home, shortly after, was again changed, the elder Dickens being placed upon duty in Chatham Dockyard; and the house where he lived in Chatham, which had a plain-looking whitewashed plaster front and a small garden before and behind, and was in St Mary's Place, otherwise called the Brook, and next door to a Baptist meeting-house called Providence Chapel, of which a Mr Giles he presently mentioned was minister. Charles at this time was between four and five years old; and here he stayed till he was nine. Here the most durable of his early impressions were revived; and the associations that were around him when he died were those which at the outset of his life had affected him most strongly.

The house called Gadshill Place stands on the strip of highest ground in the main road between Rochester and Gravesend. Very often had we travelled past it together, many years before it became his home; and never without some allusion to what he told me when first I saw it in his company, that amid the recollections connected with his childhood it held always a prominent place, for, upon first seeing it as he came from Chatham with his father, and looking up at it with much admiration, he had been promised that he might himself live in it or in some such house when he came to be a man, if he would only work hard enough. Which for a long time was his ambition...

JOHN FORSTER

AFTER READING

1 Write down three facts from John Forster's biography. Write down any details which might be called 'opinion'.

2 How successful is the extract in making you want to read on? Why?

Dickens

— Prologue —

CHARLES DICKENS was dead. He lay on a narrow green sofa – but there was room enough for him, so spare had he become – in the dining room of Gad's Hill Place. He had died in the house which he had first seen as a small boy and which his father had pointed out to him as a suitable object of his ambitions; so great was his father's hold upon his life that, forty years later, he had bought it. Now he had gone. It was customary to close the blinds and curtains, thus enshrouding the corpse in darkness before its last journey to the tomb; but in the dining room of Gad's Hill the curtains were pulled apart and on this June day the bright sunshine streamed in, glittering on the large mirrors around the room. The family beside him knew how he enjoyed the light, how he needed the light; and they understood, too, that none of the conventional sombreness of the late Victorian period – the year was 1870 – had ever touched him.

All the lines and wrinkles which marked the passage of his life were now erased in the stillness of death. He was not old – he died in his fifty-eighth year – but there had been signs of premature ageing on a visage so marked and worn; he had acquired, it was said, a "sarcastic look". But now all that was gone and his daughter, Katey, who watched him as he lay dead, noticed how there once more emerged upon his face "beauty and pathos". It was that "long-forgotten" look which he describes again and again in his fiction. He sees it in Oliver Twist, in the dead face which returns to the "... long forgotten expression of sleeping infancy", and in that same novel he connects "the rigid face of the corpse and the calm sleep of the child". In Master Humphrey's death, too, there was something "so strangely and indefinably allied to youth". It was the look he recorded in William Dorrit's face in death; it was the look which he saw in the faces of the corpses on view in the Paris Morgue. This connection between death and infancy is one that had haunted him: sleep, repose, death, infancy, innocence, oblivion, are the words that formed a circle for him, bringing him back to the place from which he had begun. Here, in Gad's Hill, close to the town in which he had lived as a small child, here in the house which his father had once shown him; here the circle was complete.

A death mask was made. He had always hated masks. He had been frightened by one as a child and throughout his writing there is this refrain – "What a very alarming thing it would be to find somebody with a mask on...hiding bolt upright in a corner and pretending not to be alive!" The mask was an emblem of Charles Dickens's particular fear; that the dead are only pretending to be dead, and that they will suddenly spring up into violent life. He had a fear of the dead, and of all inanimate things, rising up around him to claim him; it is the fear of the pre-eminently solitary child and solitary man. But was there not also here some anticipation of the final quietus? The mask was made, and he was laid in his oak coffin. This wooden resting place was then covered with scarlet geraniums; they were Charles Dickens's favourite flowers and in the final picture of the corpse covered with blossom we can see a true representation of Dickens's own words echoing across the years – "Brighten it, brighten it, brighten it!" He always wanted colour about him, and he was notorious for his own vivid costumes. Especially in youth: and, on the wall above the coffin, his family placed a portrait of him as a young man. It was no doubt that painted by Daniel Maclise, and it shows the Dickens of 1839 looking up from his desk, his eyes ablaze as if in anticipation of the glory that was to come. Georgina Hogarth, his sister-in-law, cut a lock of hair from his head. On his prior instructions, his horse was shot. And so Charles Dickens lay.

The news of his death, in that age of swift communication, soon travelled around the world. In America Longfellow wrote that "I never knew an author's death to cause such general mourning. It is no exaggeration to say that this whole country is stricken with grief. But this is perhaps no surprise in a country which had greeted the arrival of the latest sheets of *The Old Curiosity Shop* with cries of "Is Little Nell dead?" Carlyle wrote, "It is an event world-wide, a *unique* of talents suddenly extinct..." And at once a certain aspect of his significance was seen clearly; as the *Daily News* wrote on 10 June, the day after his death, "He was emphatically the novelist of his age. In his pictures of contemporary life posterity will read, more clearly than in contemporary records, the character of nineteenth-century life."

PETER ACKROYD

AFTER READING

1 Write down three facts from Peter Ackroyd's biography. Write down any details which might be called 'opinion'.

2 How successful is the extract in making you want to read on? Why?

COMPARE

Discussion

1   John Forster starts his biography at the start of Charles Dickens's life. Peter Ackroyd begins with his death. What are the advantages and disadvantages of each approach?

2   Pick out one sentence from John Forster's extract which is typical of the style you would expect in a biography. Then pick out a sentence from Peter Ackroyd's which seems more typical of a novel.

3   In pairs, have a go at rewriting one paragraph of Peter Ackroyd's extract in a more factual style. What kinds of words and sentences have you had to cut?

Assignments

1   Write a brief biography of someone you know (it might be a member of your family or someone in your class). Don't try to give the whole life-story; instead start by interviewing them about a key moment in their life. Make notes, or record this on to cassette. Then write an account of what you have been told. Ask the subject to read it through and to make a few comments about the accuracy of what you wrote. Were there any points of misunderstanding or incorrect emphasis?

2   Using an encyclopaedia or a biographical dictionary, look up a famous person you are interested in. From the brief outline of the life given in the reference book, write your own profile of the person. Add any other information you know about the person, and say what you like or admire about him or her.

3   Write a critical comparison of the two Dickens extracts, arguing in favour of whichever biographical style you prefer. You might refer to the following:
- facts learnt about Charles Dickens
- differences in style (vocabulary, sentence structure, levels of description, use of dialogue)
- balance of facts versus description.

WIDER READING

Short Stories
Short-story writers have to work especially hard to gain the reader's attention and hold it for the duration of their tale. This selection provides an opportunity to study some first-rate storytellers at work:

Penelope Lively, *Pack of Cards*; Robert Westall (ed), *Ghost Stories*; Roy Blatchford (ed), *Shorties: The Penguin Complete Saki*; Graham Greene, *Collected Short Stories*; Edna O'Brien, *Returning*.

Biography/Autobiography
The single most useful volume for finding good biographies and autobiographies is *The Bloomsbury Good Reading Guide to Biography and Autobiography*, (ed) Kenneth and Valerie McLeish.

AFTER READING

1 In essay form, present a personal selection of some of the best novel and short-story openings you have read.

2 Write an account of a biography or autobiography you have enjoyed reading, commenting on its structure and style as well as on the content.

PERSUASION

Rhetoric *n.* **1.** the study of the technique of using language effectively. **2.** the art of using speech to persuade, influence or please; oratory.

Collins English Dictionary

Language is a powerful and influential medium. It can make us believe that war is bracing and attractive, persuade us to buy a particular product, or induce us to support a certain charity.
- *Look at some persuasive language in action – how does it achieve its effects?*
- *Could a skilful speaker entice us to buy or do <u>anything</u>?*

THE GLORY OF WAR

■ Each of the following three passages presents an argument for going to war. The first is from an Army Recruitment advertisement published in the USA.

READING SKILLS
Analysing language

| Reading aloud |

The American Soldier

Today's American soldiers are the inheritors of over two hundred years of tradition. Courage, perseverance and the willingness to accept challenge, no matter how demanding, are part of their legacy.

The American soldier won us a free Nation. The soldier, down through the days of war and years of peace, has borne the brunt of preserving this Nation. He has met challenge after challenge. He has overcome each in its turn. The days of challenge have not ended, nor has the need for men to come forward to accept the demands of responsibility, leadership and opportunity in the Combat Arms of today's Army.

Here is the proving ground for men. Here is where you can push yourself to the limits of skill, strength and stamina. And then exceed those limits. Here is where you can honour the traditions of the combat soldier and, in your time, add to them.

The days of challenge have not ended. Every minute of every day people like you are testing themselves against the demands made on them by the life of the combat soldier. If you can see yourself meeting the challenges you just read about, see your Army Representative. There's a place for you, where you can carry on the traditions of the American combat soldier.

Join the people who've joined the Army

- -

HENRY V

Act Three
Scene I – *France. Before Harfleur*

Alarum. Enter the KING, EXETER, BEDFORD GLOUCESTER, *and* SOLDIERS *with scaling-ladders*

King

> Once more unto the breach, dear friends, once
>   more;
> Or close the wall up with our English dead!
> In peace there's nothing so becomes a man
> As modest stillness and humility:
> But when the blast of war blows in our ears,
> Then imitate the action of the tiger:
> Stiffen the sinews, conjure up the blood,
> Disguise fair nature with hard-favour'd rage;
> Then lend the eye a terrible aspect;
> Let it pry through the portage of the head
> Like the brass cannon; let the brow o'erwhelm it
> As fearfully as doth a galled rock

AFTER READING

1 List three points that the writer make to put his argument across.

2 What do you notice about the kinds of words and sentences the writer uses?

■ Shakespeare's Henry V is at a critical point in the Battle of Agincourt when he stops to encourage his troops to fight on. In the scene which follows Henry's famous speech we see how the soldiers react to it.

O'erhang and jutty his confounded base,
Swill'd with the wild and wasteful ocean.
Now set the teeth and stretch the nostril wide;
Hold hard the breath, and bend up every spirit
To his full height! On, on, you noblest English,
Whose blood is fet from fathers of war-proof
Fathers that, like so many Alexanders,
Have in these parts from morn till even fought,
And sheath'd their swords for lack of argument.
Dishonour not your mothers; now attest
That those whom you call'd fathers did beget you!
Be copy now to men of grosser blood,
And teach them how to war. And you, good yeomen,
Whose limbs were made in England, show us here
The mettle of your pasture; let us swear
That you are worth your breeding – which I doubt not;
For there is none of you so mean and base
That hath not noble lustre in your eyes.
I see you stand like greyhounds in the slips,
Straining upon the start. The game's afoot!
Follow your spirit, and upon this charge
Cry, 'God for Harry, England, and Saint George!'

Exeunt. Alarum, and chambers go off

Scene II – *Before Harfleur*
Enter NYM, BARDOLPH, PISTOL, *and* BOY

Bardolph
On, on, on, on, on! to the breach, to the breach!

Nym
Pray thee, Corporal, stay – the knocks are too hot, and,
for mine own part, I have not a case of lives. The
humour of it is too hot, that is the very plain-song of it.

Pistol
The plainsong is most just; for humours do abound.
Knocks go and come; God's vassals drop and die;
        And sword and shield,
        In bloody field,
        Doth win immortal fame.

Boy
Would I were in an alehouse in London! I would give
all my fame for a pot of ale, and safety.

WILLIAM SHAKESPEARE

AFTER READING

1 Why do you think Henry refers so much to 'England' and the 'English'? What persuasive technique is he using here?

2 What does Scene II, with Nym, Bardolf, Pistol and the boy suggest? Have they been stirred by Henry's rhetoric?

■ This poem is written by a Nigerian poet who has different reasons for going to war.

A WARRIOR'S LAMENT

Now on the battlefield
I know what faces me.
It is death; my death.
I do not hate those I fight;
It is their deeds I hate.
Those I am fighting for do not love me;
My death shall not grieve them,
Nor shall it bring them joy.
No law compels me to fight;
None has sent me out to fight
Except my deep love for my own.
My friends want me to desert the field,
That I may not perish in battle.
But they forget: A serpent
Does not attack a child before its mother's eyes.
It is true that my mother, my mother's offspring,
My friends, the beautiful girl I want to marry,
Are worrying themselves to death about me;
Still I shall not leave the battlefield
For the enemy to march them away before my eyes.
I have left home to live in the bush.
The hunting I do now is the shooting of fellow humans.
I have become a beast of the forest
That I may bring peace to my own.
I am in the midst of battle now.
Listen to what is resounding in the forest where I stand!
Kwaku-kwaku is our morning greeting;
Unudum! Unudum! the song of the guns!
As it sounds and resounds I become uncaring about life,
And strum my gun like a guitar.
When all the gunfire stops
I lift up my head,
I laugh;
When I turn around
The companions of my morning meal
Have become corpses.
I know one day it will be my turn.
I have already seen my death.
One day I will lie like my friends who lie here.

Vultures, termites, and other creatures of the forest
Shall hold a conference on top of me.
My bones will lie scattered in the bush.
When some farmer clears the forest
He'll gather up my skull and bones;
When he burns the debris of the forest he'll burn me.
When crops grow they'll grow on my bones.
No maiden shall kiss my lips
For the earth, it is not kissed.
Thus my life shall come to an end.
And my companions and my kin,
They shall lift up their eyes forever,
Up the road at the horizon,
Looking for one that shall never return.
And the last we shall see of each other
Was before I departed for war.
The next time we set eyes on each other
Shall be in the land of rest.

NNAMDI OLEBARA
translated from the Igbo by Chinweizu

AFTER READING

1 How would you summarise the warrior's message? How persuasive is it?

2 Think of a word which best describes the speaker's *tone*.

COMPARE

Discussion

1 In groups, prepare a reading of the extracts in styles which you think are most likely to convince your audience. You might, for example, imagine the US Army text as a radio or TV commercial.

2 Which of the extracts is:
• most powerful
• most personal
• most detailed
• most persuasive?
Find evidence to support your answers.

3 Look again at each passage, and make a list of characteristics to describe the *audience* they are addressing. Then compare what these listeners/readers have in common.

4 Pick out one sentence or phrase from each passage which best captures the main point its speaker is making.

Assignments

1 Write a response to the US Army recruiting leaflet, using a similar rhetorical style, but this time encouraging people *not* to join the army.

2 Look closely again at Henry V's speech. Some critics have suggested that even though the King is rousing his men to fight, the speech could also be interpreted as having *anti*-war elements. Find evidence in the speech to support this view. Which interpretation do you agree with?

3 Each passage presents a different view of war. Write a personal response to each of them, saying which you found most interesting, and which was most and least persuasive. Provide evidence from the texts in support of your views.

PLEASE GIVE GENEROUSLY

■ The two advertisements which follow have both appeared in national newspapers accompanied by striking and disturbing photographs. Here, in order to examine the impact of the words, the pictures have not been included. Compare their effect with an extract from Heathcote Williams's poem on the history of whaling.

They took his teeth.
They took his claws.
Now they're going for his throat.

This bear, like many others in Pakistan, is being set upon by savage dogs as a spectator sport.

His teeth and claws have been pulled out and his nose drilled through to accommodate a rope.

And to make things even more unfair, he is tethered to the ground during the fight.

As part of the World Society for the Protection of Animals, the Libearty Campaign is dedicated to stamping out this illegal activity.

Bear-baiting is barbaric. Just £5 will help us enforce the law and bring the cruelty to a stop.

Libearty

The world campaign for bears

WSPA

■ The next advertisement is by the RSPCA.

BEFORE THEY'RE ROASTED IN GARLIC AND ROSEMARY THEY'RE SOAKED IN URINE AND EXCREMENT.

The trucks that carry livestock across Europe hold up to 800 sheep at a time.

The journeys can last over twenty-four hours, but the animals' bladders cannot. They begin to urinate and excrete inside the lorry.

One sheep produces around a litre of urine and 700 grammes of faeces a day.

And so do the other 799.

Since they are trapped in such a confined space their fleeces quickly become coated in droppings.

For the rest of the trip they're wet, cold and some even suffer skin burns.

Eventually the urinating stops, but only because the animals are given no water in transit.

The size of continental trucks means that unfamiliar flocks are often mixed together (an unsettling experience for any animal).

In the crush the weaker sheep lose their footing, fall to the floor and are trampled by the others.

Some die.

And all this happens so European meat traders can squeeze a little more profit from their livestock.

The sheep could be slaughtered close to their farms, refrigerated and then transported (a method favoured by many farmers).

But offal and hides fetch a slightly higher price abroad and freshly killed meat is also at a premium, so the practice continues.

At least until the law is changed.   **RSPCA**

STOP
THE NEEDLESS TRANSPORTATION
OF ANIMALS

Please phone the RSPCA for a free information pack and to find out what further action you can take.

RSPCA

AFTER READING

1 What would you say is the ratio of facts to opinion in this advertisement (e.g. 50:50)?

2 On a scale of 1 (least) to 5 (most) how effective do you find the advert in persuading you to support the campaign?

■ This poem extract, like the advertisments, has a message to convey.

Whale Nation

On deck, the skull, jaw-bones, ribs, spine and pelvis
Are dismembered with chain-saws,
Then ground down, and shovelled into the bone-cookers;
Melted and milled into chicken-feed and fertilisers.

From a whale who was pregnant,
The unborn are dragged into the meat-boilers
With huge hooks slung into their blow-holes.

The inner organs are towed into other boilers
To be distilled into pharmaceuticals.
The skin is collected from the slipways for glycerine.
The belly blubber is reserved for a delicacy known as
'whale bacon'.
The jaw cartilage is pickled.
The tail-flukes are frozen, to be eaten raw.

The floating factory has done little but exchange twenty
thousand gallons of petroleum
For twenty thousand gallons of animal oil.
Foreign currency has been acquired.
The odd fact that no whale has been found with a serious
pathological disease,
No whale has ever been found suffering from cancerous
tumours,
Is overlooked.

Yet civilisation was built on the back of the whale:
Coastal settlements followed the presence of whales;
Shore-stations near the whaling grounds became cities.

HEATHCOTE WILLIAMS

AFTER READING

1 Is the content of this poem entirely factual, or are there some lines which you would describe as opinion? Give examples.

2 What can you tell about Heathcote Williams's attitude
• to whales?
• to humans?

COMPARE

Discussion

1 Which of the passages:

- has the most powerful effect on you
- uses the strongest language?

Provide evidence for your answers.

2 Discuss who you think the passages are aimed at – which specific readership?

3 How could the two charity advertisements improve their power to persuade you?

Assignments

1 Take the facts from Heathcote Williams's poem and use them to make an advertisement for a charity opposed to whaling. Use the techniques you have noted in the two charity advertisements.

2 Write an analysis of the two advertisements, comparing:

- their use of layout
- their headlines (do they catch your eye?)
- their use of factual information
- their persuasive techniques
- their language.

Conclude by saying which of the charities you would be more likely to support and why.

3 Choose one of the advertisements, and rewrite it for a different readership (e.g. children aged ten to fourteen). How would you persuade them to support your campaign by signing a petition? How would you change the language of the advertisement? Once you have rewritten the advertisement, write a paragraph explaining the decisions you have made.

EIGHTEENTH-CENTURY PERSUASION

■ In 1729 extreme poverty was leading to the deaths of many people in Ireland, but the British Government did little to improve the situation. The writer Jonathan Swift (the author of *Gulliver's Travels*) wrote a proposal for solving the problem: the children of the poor people, he mockingly suggested, should be eaten.

A MODEST
PROPOSAL
FOR

Preventing the Children of poor People in Ireland, from being a Burden to their Parents or Country; and for making them beneficial to the Publick.

Written in the Year 1729

...I AM assured by our Merchants, that a Boy or a Girl before twelve Years old, is no saleable Commodity; and even when they come to this Age, they will not yield above Three Pounds, or Three Pounds and half a Crown at most, on the Exchange; which cannot turn to Account either to the Parents or the Kingdom; the Charge of Nutriment and Rags, having been at least four Times that Value.

I SHALL now therefore humbly propose my own Thoughts; which I hope will not be liable to the least Objection.

I HAVE been assured by a very knowing *American* of my Acquaintance in *London*; that a young healthy Child, well nursed, is, at a Year old, a most delicious, nourishing, and wholesome Food; whether *Stewed, Roasted, Baked,* or *Boiled*; and, I make no doubt, that it will equally serve in a *Fricasie*, or *Ragoust*.

I DO therefore humbly offer it to *publick Consideration*, that of the Hundred and Twenty Thousand Children, already computed, Twenty thousand may be reserved for Breed: whereof only one Fourth Part to be Males; which is more than we allow to *Sheep, black Cattle,* or *Swine*; and my Reason is, that these Children are seldom the Fruits of Marriage, *a Circumstance not much regarded by our Savages*; therefore, *one Male* will be

sufficient to serve *four Females*. That the remaining
Hundred thousand, may, at a Year old, be offered in Sale
to the *Persons of Quality and Fortune*, through the
Kingdom; always advising the Mother to let them suck
plentifully in the last Month, so as to render them plump,
and fat for a good Extent, and shall take in the whole
Number of Infants at a certain Age, who are born of
Parents, in effect as little able to support them, as those
who demand our Charity in the Streets....

I CAN think of no one Objection, that will possibly
be raised against this Proposal; unless it should be urged,
that the Number of People will be thereby much lessened
in the Kingdom. This I freely own; and it was indeed one
principal Design in offering it to the World. I desire the
Reader will observe, that I calculate my Remedy for this
one individual Kingdom of IRELAND, and *for no other
that ever was, is, or I think ever can be upon Earth.* Therefore,
let no man talk to me of other Expedients: Of taxing our
Absentees at five Shillings a Pound: *Of using neither
Cloaths, nor Houshold Furniture except what is of our own
Growth and Manufacture.*

I PROFESS, in the Sincerity of my Heart, that I have
not the least personal Interest, in endeavouring to
promote this necessary Work; having no other Motive
than the *publick Good of my Country, by advancing our
Trade, providing for Infants, relieving the Poor, and giving
some Pleasure to the Rich.* I have no Children, by which I
can propose to get a single Penny; the youngest being
nine Years old, and my Wife past Child-bearing.

JONATHAN SWIFT

AFTER READING

1 Discuss what you consider
to be the main points that
Jonathan Swift is making.
Make a list of them.

2 After a first reading, how
difficult on a scale of 1
(least) to 5 (most) do you find
the language of the extract?

Discussion

1 What clues are there, in the language and the content, that this Proposal was written long ago? In pairs, find five examples.

2 What clues are there that the Proposal is not intended to be serious?

3 How would you describe the writer's tone: comic, angry, pompous, agressive, concerned, helpful?

Find evidence from the extract to support your choice.

Assignments

1 Write Jonathan Swift's proposal in modern English, perhaps as a speech for an MP in Parliament, or as a letter to a newspaper.

2 Imagine that someone has read Swift's proposal and has taken it seriously. They are appalled by what he suggests. Write the letter that they might write to Swift objecting to the cruelty of his idea.

3 Write your own 'Modest Proposal' suggesting ways to ease one of the following universal problems:

- violence
- drug abuse
- global warming

Decide whether to make it serious or funny, and write it as a speech or pamphlet.

WIDER READING

Books which include persuasive speeches
David Cannadine (ed), *The Speeches of Winston Churchill*; Brian MacArthur, *The Penguin Book of Twentieth-Century Speeches*.

Books which seek solutions to world problems
Bernadette Vallely, *1001 Ways to Save the Planet*; Larry Kramer, *Reports from the Holocaust*; Bob Geldof, *Is That It?*

AFTER READING

1 Choose two or three speeches that you find particularly enticing, and write a personal response discussing their effect.

2 Discuss the work of one writer who interests you, together with his or her proposals to improve the world.

Acknowledgments

We should like to thank the following authors and publishers for permission to reproduce copyright material:

Extract from *The Go-Between* by LP Hartley (Hamish Hamilton, 1957) copyright © LP Hartley, 1957, reproduced by permission of Hamish Hamilton Ltd, p.3; Hutchinson, extract from *Right Ho, Jeeves* by PG Wodehouse, p.8; Today, 'A Crying Shame' by Penny Wark, p.11; The *Sun*, 'Bingo £10,000' and 'Knife Fiend Blown Away', p.12, and 'Honesty's a Winner', p.13; 'Olorum Nimbe' from *Oral Literature in Africa* edited by Ruth Finnegan (1970), by permission of Oxford University Press, p.15; Hodder Headline, 'Man Overboard!' by Winston Churchill, p.24; Tim Crawley, 'Cold Hands', p.28, and 'The Writing of *Cold Hands*', p.35; 'Instant Horror' by Calum Watson & Mike Moustafi, © the *Guardian*, p.39; 'Michael Jackson' from *A Dictionary of Twentieth-Century Biography* (1992), ed. Asa Briggs, by permission of Oxford University Press, p.43; 'A Glance in Michael's Mirror' by Catherine Bennett, © the *Guardian*, p.44; Bantam Press, extract from *Nancy Reagan: The Unauthorized Biography* by Kitty Kelley (1991) by permission of Transworld Publishers Ltd, p.46; Extract from *And When Did You Last See Your Father?* by Blake Morrison (Granta, 1993) copyright © Blake Morrison, 1993, reproduced by permission of Penguin Books Ltd, p.51; extract from 'The Prologue' from *The Canterbury Tales* by Geoffrey Chaucer, translated by Nevill Coghill (Penguin Classics 1951, fourth revised edition 1977) copyright © Nevill Coghill, 1951, 1958, 1960, 1975, 1977, reproduced by permission of Penguin Books Ltd, p.56; *The Independent*, extract from 'Boys will be Boys' by Deborah Holder, first published in *The Independent on Sunday*, p.60; East African Educational Publishers Ltd, 'Letter from a Contract Worker' by Antonio Jacunti, first published in *When the Bullets begin to Flower*, ed. Margaret Dickinson, p.74; Georgia Garrett, 'Manwatching', p.75; Somak Holidays, 'Taj Mahal and the Pink City' from the brochure *A Taste of Kenya, Tanzania, India, etc*, p.80; Rough Guides, extract from 'Trekking to Kashmir' by Liz Maudslay, p.82; Peters, Fraser and Dunlop, extract from *Icewalk* by Robert Swan, p.94; Spillers Foods, 'Popular Dog Names', p.97 and 'Popular Cat Names', p.98; NTC Business Books, extract from *NTC's Dictionary of Trade Name Origins* by Adrian Room, p.99; 'What lips my lips have kissed' by Edna St Vincent Millay from *Collected Poems*, HarperCollins, copyright 1923, 1951 by Edna St Vincent Millay and Norma Millay Ellis, reprinted by permission of Elizabeth Barnett, literary Executor; Foreign Language Press, 'Untitled' by Shu Ting from *Women of the Red Plain*, translated by Julia C Lin, p.102; Jonathan Cape, 'A Gentle Requiem' from *An African Elegy* by Ben Okri, p.103; extract from *Mother Tongue* by Bill Bryson (Hamish Hamilton, 1990) copyright © Bill Bryson, 1990, reproduced by permission of Hamish Hamilton Ltd, p.105; The University of California Press, 'The World of Doublespeak' by William Lutz from *State of the Language* (1990 edition) ed. Christopher Ricks & Leonard Michaels, copyright © 1989 The Regents of the University of California, p.108; The Society of Authors, on behalf of the Bernard Shaw estate, extract from *Pygmalion* by Bernard Shaw, p.111; extract from 'Teenagers More Tolerant of Crime' by Richard Spencer © the *Telegraph* plc, London 1993, p.117; extract from 'A Wrong Turn in Teaching Morality' by Peter Mullen, by courtesy of the *Yorkshire Post*, p.118; William Heinemann Ltd, extract from *To Kill A Mockingbird* by Harper Lee, p.121; Vanguard Press, 'Justice', first published in *African Voices* ed. Peggy Rutherford, p.123; Faber and Faber Ltd, extract from *The Lord of the Flies* by William Golding, p.125; *Our Country's Good* copyright © 1988 by Timberlake Wertenbaker based on the novel *The Playmaker* by Thomas Keneally © 1987 The Serpentine Publishing Company Pty, published by Hodder & Stoughton and Septre, and reprinted by permission of Michael Imson Playwrights Ltd, 28 Almeida Street, London, N1 1TD, p.129; Anthony Shield Associated Ltd, 'Do you know why you're doing it?' by Alan K, p.135; Peter Walker, 'How to be a Writer', published in the *Yorkshire Evening Press*, p.137; Clarefen Ltd, extract from *The Writing School Guide to Writing the Short Story* by Roy Lomax, p.139; Longman Group UK Ltd, extract from *Jane Eyre*, retold by Sue Ullstein (Longman Classics Series), p.147; Oxford Bookworms series, extract from *Jane Eyre*, retold by Clare West (1990), by permission of Oxford University Press, p.148; Watson, Little Ltd, extract from 'Paradise Illustrated: A Sequence' by DJ Enright, published by Oxford University Press in *The Collected Poems of DJ Enright*, p.154; Sinclair Stevenson, extract from *Dickens* by Peter Ackroyd, p.157; The US Army Recruitment Station, 'The American Soldier', p.160; Di Negro Press, 'A Warrior's Lament' by Nnamdi Olebara from *Fires of Africa* ed. Naiwda Osalon, p.163; Libearty Campaign, WSPA, 'They took his teeth...', p.165; RSPCA, 'Before they're roasted...', p.166; Jonathan Cape, extract from 'Whale Nation' by Heathcote Williams, p.167.

The authors and publishers would like to thank the following for permission to reproduce illustrations:

Joy Bennett, pp 61, 86, 91; Camera Press, pp 11, 44, 46, 112; The Dickens House Museum, London, p.155; Dover Books, pp 6, 8, 14, 16, 19, 20, 21, 23, 27, 28, 42, 58, 63, 75, 79, 96, 97, 98, 101, 104, 110, 111, 124, 125, 130, 131, 133, 136, 143, 146, 151, 158, 160, 168, 170, 171; Mary Evans Picture Library, pp 50, 56, 89, 92, 93; Gay Galsworthy, p.70; The *Guardian*, p.41; Hammer Film Productions Ltd, p.18; Richard Hayes, p.80; Hulton Deutsch, pp 51, 153, 161; *Nightmare on Elm Street II: Freddy's Revenge* © 1985 New Line Productions, Inc. All rights reserved. Photo by Michelle Singer. Photo appears courtesy of New Line Productions, Inc, p.39; The Shakespeare Birthplace Trust, p.77.